COSTANTINO GUERRA

FLORENCE

History and Masterpieces

270 COLOR PHOTOGRAPHS

CITY MAP

BONECHI EDIZIONI "IL TURISMO"

© Copyright 2005 by Bonechi - Edizioni "Il Turismo" S.r.l.
Via G. Di Vittorio, 31 - 50145 Florence
Tel. +39-055 37.57.39/342.45.27
Fax +39-055 37.47.01
E-mail: bbonechi@dada.it
        info@bonechionline.com
http://www.bonechionline.com
All right reserved
Printed in Italy

Publishing manager: Barbara Bonechi
Layout: Sabrina Menicacci
Cover: Paola Rufino
Photo credits: Archives of the Publishing House;
Nicola Grifoni (Florence); Nicolò Orsi Battaglini (Florence); Marco Rabatti (Florence)
The photo on page 30 (below) was kindly granted by Cassa di Risparmio di Firenze.
Photolitography: Puntoeacapo, Florence
Print: Lito Terrazzi, Florence

ISBN: 88-7204-590-8

Historical Note

The origins of Florence go back to the Etruscan epoch, when Fiesole dominated the valley from its hill. Groups of inhabitants went down to the banks of the Arno to found a village, modest, but destined to thrive, thanks to its favourable position on the direct line of communication between the north and south of Italy; altough this did make it more vulnerable by enemy attack and invasion.

The Romans soon founded a colony here with the auspicious name of *Florentia* (that is, destinated to flourish). Already in the 2nd century BC the new municipality has acquired a position of pre-eminence among the cities of the Roman *Tuscia*.

The town survived the Dark Ages to emerge slowly in the Carolingian epoch. First the feud of the Marquises of Tuscany, among whom Ugo and Matilda should be recorded, from the 11th century onwards Florence began to acquire greater and greater autonomy; in 1115, after the struggles against the simoniacal clergy and the feudal lords of the surrounding neighbourhood, the Florentine Commune had virtually come into being; ten years later the new state defeated her rival, Fiesole.

▼ *Panorama of the city.*

3

◀ *Roman sarcophagus in the courtyard of the Cathedral Museum.*

Soon, inside the city, now surrounded by a new circle of walls, the first clashes began to take place between immigrant overlords and the artistan class, organised into the extremely powerful Guilds and Trade Corporations.

These clashes created the two factions of the *Guelphs* (who supported the Pope) and the *Ghibellines* (who favoured the Emperor) with the distinct prevalence of the former. After the end of the 13th century the Guelphs themselves divided into two parties of "black" and "white", which has split up on the basis of a long-standing rivarly; the black party, supported by the Pope, sent the white partisans into exile in 1303; these included Dante Alighieri.

In the meantime Florence was becoming more powerful, fighting against rival cities (Pistoia, Arezzo, Volterra, Siena) and expanding her territory. Also in the cultural and economic fields, at the turn of the 13th-14th century, she was becoming one of the most important centres in Italy. This was the period of the great companies of bankers and merchants, when the wool and silk industries were flourishing. In 1348 there was a terrible outbreak of plague, described by Boccaccio at the beginning of the *Decameron*.

The last decades of the 14th century saw increasingly violent clashes between the *popolo grasso*, the rich middle class which ruled the state by means of the Guilds, and the *popolo minuto* or working class. The struggle came to a head in the *Tumulto dei Ciompi* (humble carders in the Wool Guild) by means of which the lower classes of the citizenry came to power (1378). But soon afterwards the oligarchy heades by the Albizi regained the ascendancy by supporting the small populace; the rich Medici family was acquiring increasing political importance, and soon the rule of the Signoria was established, although republican appearances were preserved. Cosimo the Elder, who founded the Medici rule, was succeeded by Lorenzo the Magnificent, a shrewd statesman and a great patron of the arts.

The century that culminated in the rule of the Magnificent (died 1492) is one of the most brilliant in Florentine history, especially in the field of culture and art; it was the cen-

◀ *The Guild Hall of the Wool Merchants.*

▼ *Cosimo the Elder, by Pontormo*

tury of Humanism and the great art of the Renaissance.

Between the end of the 15th and the early 16th century the city had a free Republican government, after the expulsion of Piero, the successor to Lorenzo. This period is dominated by the figure of Girolamo Savonarola. After the Medicis returned, Florence remained under their rule until 1527, when a fresh revolt restored the Republican institutions. But the Medicis, supported by the Emperor and the Pope, returned once more after a harsh siege (1530).

▲ *Lorenzo the Magnificent with the Artists, by Ottavio Vannini (Silver Museum-Palazzo Pitti).*

▼ *Savonarola's martyrdom in Piazza della Signoria, in a late 15th century painting (San Marco Museum).*

Despite the political unrest, the years between the end of the 15th century and the first decades of the 16th century were rich in great personalities in the artistic and literary fields (Michelangelo, Machiavelli, Guicciardini).

In 1569 Cosimo dei Medici, the ruler of the city, received the title of Grand Duke, which he passed on to his successors. After Cosimo his son Francesco I acceded to the government of the city; a lover of art and letters, he had little propensity for ruling.

The following century saw the beginning of the city's decline; international factors (the preponderance in Europe of the great powers of France, Austria and Spain; the shift northwards of the centres of economic power) and the lack of significant personalities among the Medici Grand Dukes, with the exception of Ferdinando II, all com-

◀ *Detail of the David, by Michelangelo.*

bined to exclude Florence, as for that matter the whole of Italy, from the category of European powers. The extinction of the dinasty with Gian Gastone (1737) and the passing of the Grand Duchy to the Lorraine family, connected with the ruling Austrian house, allowed Florence to recover a certain marginal importance in Europe.

The Lorraines ruled the Grand Duchy, except during the period of Napoleonic domination (1799-1814), until the union of Florence and Tuscany with Italy (1859). Florence was the capital of the new kingdom from 1865 to 1871. The city continued to be, as it is now, a lively artistic and cultural centre.

▼ *Picturesque view of Florence at dusk.*

Piazza del Duomo

At the dawn of the Middle Ages, the site of the Piazza was a mass of dwelling houses and public buildings. The church of Santa Reparata was built over the foundations of one of the latter in the 4th century. Three centuries later, the Baptistery was built next to the church, and this area began to be the centre of religious life in Florence. Santa Reparata became a cathedral in 1128. The church was becoming too small for its new role and increased importance – the population was in-

▲ *The Cathedral and Giotto's Bell Tower.*

creasing too – and in 1289 the Commune decided to enlarge it. This was part of an extensive rebuilding project, involving new and more extensive city walls (the Roman circle was too small), the construction of a Priors' Palace (now Palazzo Vecchio) and alterations to existing buildings such as Santa Croce, the church of the Badia, Orsanmichele, the Bargello and the Baptistery. In order to achieve a city that should be new but harmonious, one man, Arnolfo di Cambio, was given the responsibility of directing and coordinating the work. One of the greatest architects and sculptors of his time, he raised the level of the piazza (which he had re-paved), eliminating the podium on which the Baptistery had previously stood, demolished a few houses nearby, and began to build the new cathedral, for which he planned a dome and external decoration matching that of the Baptistery. The death of Arnolfo in 1302 put a stop to the work, which was resumed in 1332-34 with the construction of the Bell Tower under the direction of Giotto. The addition of a dome by Brunelleschi (1420-34) made it the impressive, dominating building that we see today (the façade dates from the 19th century).

◄ *Bird's eye view of the religious complex in Piazza del Duomo.*

◄ ▼ Tomb slaps in the crypt of Santa Reparata and St. John, detail of a fresco depicting the Passion of Christ.

The construction of the Cathedral, dedicated to Santa Maria del Fiore (St. Mary of the Flower) was begun in 1294 by Arnolfo di Cambio, chosen by the city authorities and the citizens, who wanted a cathedral not only larger than the previous church of Santa Reparata but "so sumptuous and magnificent" that it would outshine the cathedrals of rival Tuscan cities both in beauty and dimensions. The new cathedral was constructed around the older church, the simple structure and two bell towers being incorporated. Santa Reparata was finally pulled down in 1375; but the Florentines went on calling the new cathedral by the old name for a long time – the authorities had to inflict heavy fines in order to enforce the use of the new one: "Santa Maria del Fiore". The lower part of Santa Reparata, buried underneath the floor of the Duomo till quite recently, can now be visited by going down a staircase from the right aisle; it contains remains of frescoes, sculptures and tombstones, that of Filippo Brunelleschi included.

The façade was designed by a 19th century architect, Emilio De Fabris, who tried to recapture the Florentine Gothic Style. The project, which he worked on until 1871, was

◄ One of the four exedras of the Cathedral.

The façade of the Cathedral.

◀ *The Almond Door,*
in the left side of the Cathedral,
with the mosaic representing
the Annunciation,
by Domenico Ghirlandaio (1491).

continued by Luigi Del Moro, who completed it in 1887. It is divided into three sections, each of which is topped by a rose window. In the 13 tabernacles above the doorways are statues of the *Apostles*, the central position being occupied by a *Virgin and Child* by Tito Sarrocchi. In the four lower tabernacles (from left to right): a *statue of the Bishop Valeriani*, who blessed the Cathedral's first stone; *Bishop Tinacci*, who blessed the first pillar; *Pope Eugene IV*, who consecrated the church and *St. Antonius*, who blessed the façade. The partitions are sculptured with *Scenes from the Life of the Virgin* and allegorical figures representing the *Virtues*: *Temperance, Faith, Humility* and *Prudence*. In the lunette is an allegorical mosaic showing *Charity enthroned*. The central doorway, by Passaglia (1903), is decorated with the *Conception* and the *Coronation of the Virgin* and, in the lunette, *Christ, the Virgin and the patrons of the city*, by Barabino.

The stately and spacious interior of the Duomo was the scene of the fiery sermons of Savonarola and of the savage Pazzi conspiracy: on 26th April 1478 members of the Pazzi family, enemies of the Medicis, in league with Archbishop Salviati, attacked Lorenzo the Magnificent and his brother Giuliano during Mass. Lorenzo escaped, but Giuliano was killed and the conspiracy was followed by harsh repression.

▲ *The interior of the Cathedral.*

▼ *Monument to Niccolò da Tolentino,*
by Andrea del Castagno

▲ *Monument to Giovanni Acuto, by Paolo Uccello.*

Works of art of many centuries embellish the cathedral but do not mask the severity of its high ogival arches and composite pillars. On the inside of the façade is an enormous clock, painted in 1443 and decorated with four heads of *Prophets* depicted by Paolo Uccello. Also by Paolo Uccello is the fresco of the *Monument to Giovanni Acuto* (John Hawkwood) on the wall in the left aisle; beside, left, is the *Monument to Niccolò da Tolentino*, by Andrea del Castagno (1456).

▶ *Dante and the Divine Comedy,*
by Domenico di Michelino (1465).

◀ *The vault of the dome, frescoed by Vasari and Zuccari, with a depiction of the Last Judgement.*

with frescoes by Giorgio Vasari and Federico Zuccari (1572-79) representing the *Last Judgement* in five superimposed bands. Over the high altar is a wooden *Crucifix* by Benedetto da Maiano and round it is the octagonal *choir* by Baccio Bandinelli (1555), decorated with bas-reliefs.

Behind the altar on the right is the **Old Sacristy** with an *Ascension* in terracotta by Luca della Robbia in the lunette over the entrance. Directly opposite on the other side of the Tribune is the **New Sacristy**, with a fine bronze door by Luca della Robbia, Michelozzo and Maso di Bartolomeo (1445-69). In the lunette, *Resurrection*, also by Luca. Inside the sacristy, splendid fifteenth-century *inlaid cupboards*. In the chapel at the end of the apse is a bronze urn by Ghiberti with *Relics of Saint Zanobius.*

Above the large octagonal tribune is the *dome* by Brunelleschi. A competition for its construction was announced in 1418. The difficulty of this task was immediately evident, for traditional building techniques were inadequate. Brunelleschi invented an original system of mobile centres which superseded the usual one of fixed structures starting from the ground (clearly impossible to use owing to the enormous dimensions of the building) and so succeeded in defeating Lorenzo Ghiberti, his eternal rival, who also took part in the competition. The dome and the lantern were completed in 1434. The dome is based on a massive octagonal drum, has marble ribbing and is covered by red tiles baked in the kilns at Impruneta. The interior is decorated

▶ *The choir of the Cathedral.*

▲ *The dome of the Cathedral.*

▲ *The Loggia del Bigallo.*

Giotto's Bell Tower

The building of this tower began in 1334 under the direction of Giotto, after a fire had destroyed the old bell tower of Santa Reparata. Giotto died in 1337, when the base of the tower had been completed; after him work was directed by Andrea Pisano and Francesco Talenti, who brought it to conclusion (although the original plan included a spire which was never built). The building is of remarkable grace and elegance; the structure lightens and lengthens as it rises, becoming complex with marble insets and fine tracery.
The bas-reliefs on the base (the originals are in the Cathedral Museum) were carved by Andrea Pisano and his workmen under the supervision of Giotto.

Loggia del Bigallo

This was built between 1352 and 1358 by Alberto Arnoldi, in elegant Gothic style, as a shelter for the town's waifs and orphans (Innocents). Its façade, facing the baptistery, has three tabernacles with the statues of *St. Peter Martyr*, the *Virgin and Child* and *St. Lucy*.
Inside is a fine collection of works of art, with frescoes detached from the building and pieces by Ghirlandaio, Arnoldi and the schools of Botticelli and Verrocchio.

BAPTISTERY

Dante's "Bel San Giovanni" (Fair St. John) the religious building most beloved by the Florentines, was perhaps started in the 5th century, but the work done in the 11th and 12th centuries made it the most important monument of Romanesque architecture in Florence. Its regular octagonal form, the symmetrical distribution of the external decoration and the harmonic

▲ *The Baptistery* and *Christ, detail of the mosaics decorating the interior of the dome.*

▶ *Bronze panels from the Door of Paradise*
with the Story of Noah
and the Story of Joshua.

▼ **The famous Door of Paradise, by Lorenzo Ghiberti.**

*Creation of Adam and Eve
Original sin
Expulsion from Paradise*

*Adam and Eve with their sons,
Cain and Abel
Man's first labour:
Abel keeping sheep
and Cain ploughing
Cain kills Abel
Curse of Cain,
the first act of justice*

*Story of Noah:
Noah's family leaves the ark
after the Flood
Noah gives thanks to the Lord
who sends a rainbow as
a sign of peace.
Drunkenness of Noah
Noah is derided by Ham and
covered up by Shem and Japhet*

*Story of Abraham:
Sarah at the entrance
to the tent
Apparition of the angels
to Abraham
Abraham and Isaac
on the mountain
The Angel stays
Abraham's hand
as he is about to sacrifice Isaac*

*Story of Jacob and Esau:
Esau trades his birthright
for a plate of lentils
Isaac sends Esau hunting
Jacob throws a goat-skin
around his neck
Isaac mistakes Jacob for Esau
and gives him his blessing
Jacob leaves his father's house*

*Story of Joseph:
Joseph is sold to the merchants
and brought before Pharaoh
Interpretation
of Pharaoh's dream
The golden cup
in Benjamin's bag
Joseph reveals himself to
his brothers and forgives them
Joseph meets Jacob*

*Story of Moses:
Moses receives the Tablets
of the Law on Mount Sinai
Aaron waits halfway down
the mountain
The Hebrews, terrified
by the thunder and lightning
await Moses' return
at the foot of the mountain*

*Story of Joshua:
Joshua and the Hebrews
cross the Jordan,
which recedes before the Ark
The Hebrews gather twelve
stones for commemoration
The walls of Jericho fall
at the sound of the
Angels' seven trumpets*

*Story of Saul and David:
Saul defeats the Philistines
David smites Goliath
David carries Goliath's head
before the cheering crowd,
back to Jerusalem*

*King Solomon
ceremoniously receives
the Queen of Sheba
in the Temple of Jerusalem*

Lorenzo Ghiberti

Vittorio Ghiberti

blending of marble were, for centuries, an architectural ideal for artists of the stature of Arnolfo, Giotto, Brunelleschi, Leon Battista Alberti, Leonardo and Michelangelo. It has three magnificent bronze doors. The **South Door** is by Andrea Pisano (c. 1330): it consists of 28 panels illustrating the *Life of the Baptist*; the bronze cornice is by Vittorio Ghiberti (son of Lorenzo, 1452).

The **North Door** is by Lorenzo Ghiberti, cast between 1403 and 1424, after winning a competition in which Brunelleschi also took part; the 28 panels represent episodes from the *Life of Christ*.

The **East Door**, the famous *Door of Paradise*, is also by Lorenzo Ghiberti (1425-1452); it is composed of 10 gilded bronze panels, with complex *Scenes from the Old Testament* crowded with figures. The smooth pyramidal roof-covering is topped by a lantern.

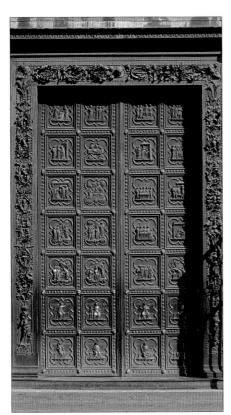

The South Door, by Andrea Pisano (14th century) and *detail of one of twenty-eight panels representing St. John baptising the Christ.*

The interior of the Baptistery is on an octagonal plan with marble decoration and each wall divided into three by tall columns; the twin-arched windows of the women's gallery open above the trabeation. A *Baptismal Font*, mentioned by Dante in the Divine Comedy, used to stand in the centre of the fine inlaid marble floor but was removed in the 16th century by Buontalenti, by order of Grand Duke Francesco I. Against the wall are: a *Baptismal Font* of the Pisan school, 14th century; the *Tomb of the anti-Pope John XXIII*, the work of Donatello and Michelozzo, commissioned by the banker Giovanni dei Medici; two Roman sarcophagi and a thirteenth-century altar. The beautiful and very striking wooden *statue of Mary Magdalene* by Donatello (1435-55), which used to be in the Baptistery, is now on view in the Cathedral Museum.

▼ *The interior of the Baptistery*

▲ *The interior of the dome with its splendid mosaics.*

The interior of the vault is covered by mosaics laid between the mid-13th and the mid-14th century by local and Venetian craftsmen (in the Middle Ages Venice was the greatest centre for mosaics). Among the most important artists who made the cartoons for the mosaics are Cimabue (*Scenes from the life of Joseph*) and Coppo di Marcovaldo (*Christ*). The subjects of the magnificent design are *Scenes from the Old and New Testaments* and the *Last Judgement*, dominated by the impressive figure of *Christ*.

These 13th and 14th century mosaics are a work of artists from the Venetian and Florentine schools. The decoration, on a gold ground, is divided into concentric bands. In the centre, round the opening of the lantern, are ornamental motifs; there follows the image of *Christ* surrounded by *Seraphs* and *Angels*; in the third band are *Scenes from the Genesis* (from the *Creation* to the *Flood*); in the fourth, *Scenes from the Life of Joseph*; in the fifth, *Scenes from the Life of Christ* and in the last one, the *Life of the Baptist*. The figure of Christ, dominating the apsidal zone, is surrounded by three superimposed bands depicting: *Angels announcing Judgement*; the *Virgin*, the *Baptist* and the *Apostles*; the *Resurrection of the Dead* and the *Division of the Blessed and the Damned*, with a terrible representation of *Hell*.

◄ *Bust of Cosimo I dei Medici, by Giovanni dell'Opera, above the entrance to the museum.*

◄ *Pietà, by Michelangelo*

Situated behind the Cathedral, the museum contains works from the Cathedral, the Bell Tower and the Baptistery. A room on the ground floor houses the sculptures from the original façade of the Cathedral, demolished in 1587, with a splendid *Virgin and Child* by Arnolfo di Cambio. The next room contains building material and mechanical devices used by Brunelleschi when building the dome. Another small room has a collection of precious reliquaries. The famous *Pietà* (Deposition) by Michelangelo is on the mezzanine. The seventy-eight year-old sculptor used a capital that came from an ancient Roman temple for this group, which he hoped would be his own grave monument in a chapel he owned in Santa Maria Maggiore in Rome.

◀ *The Drunkenness of Noah* and *the Art of Blacksmith*, marble panels from Giotto's Bell Tower, by Andrea Pisano.

◀▲ *Virgin and Child* and *St. Reparata*, two works by Arnolfo di Cambio.

◀ Statue of Boniface VIII, by Arnolfo di Cambio.

On the floor above: the two *choir galleries* by Donatello and Luca della Robbia; the Andrea Pisano marble *panels* from the bell tower; the statues of the *Baptist, Mary Magdalene* and *Habakkuk* by Donatello. Donatello's strongly realistic style in the statues of the prophets for the bell tower becomes astoundingly and exasperatedly tragic in his unique wooden Mary Magdalene. She is not the traditionally youthful beauty, which we find in most Florentine representations of the Saint, but a repentant old woman, a macabre and horrifying apparition of a being consumed by vice, sinful living and sufferings.

Other highlights include also works coming from the Baptistery as the fine *silver altar frontal* dating to the 14th-15th century with *Stories of St. John the Baptist* and the *silver altar cross*, a precious and complex work of Florentine gold craft artists, among them Betto di Francesco, Antonio del Pollaiolo and Bernardo Cennini (14th-15th century).

▼ Detail of the choir gallery, by Luca della Robbia.

▲ Jeremiah, by Donatello.

◀ *The silver altar frontal of the Baptistery with Stories of St. John the Baptist, by Verrocchio and others.*

▼ *The silver altar cross, a precious work of Betto di Francesco, Pollaiolo and Cennini.*

▶ *Habakkuk, by Donatello.*

▶ *Mary Magdalene, by Donatello.*

ORSANMICHELE

The religious and civic centres of Florence, Piazza del Duomo and Piazza della Signoria, are connected by **Via Calzaioli**, an elegant, busy shopping street, where the square bulk of Orsanmichele originally intended for secular use, was subsequently converted into a church. In 1284 the Florentine republic appointed Arnolfo to build a loggia for the collection and storage of grain, in the garden (*orto*) of the Monastery of San Michele – hence the name. This was burnt down in 1304, and rebuilt between 1337 and 1404 by Francesco Talenti and Neri di Fioravante in the slim, elegant, "decorated" Gothic style. The deposits were on the two upper floors, the grain flowed down to the loggia below through the chutes in the supporting pillars and out of the still visible openings. The external decoration was contracted out to the various city *Guilds*; each had a tabernacle with its coat of arms and the statue of its patron saint. Noteworthy, among the sculptures, are: the *Baptist* and *St. Matthew* by Ghiberti, *St. George* by Donatello (original in the Bargello) and the classical *Four Crowned Saints* by Nanni di Banco.

▼ *The Church of Orsanmichele.*

▲ *The Tabernacle of the Madonna delle Grazie, by Orcagna.*

The interior has a double nave with high cross vaults; in the right one, *Tabernacle* by Andrea Orcagna (1359), a large Gothic cusped shrine, the base of which is decorated with bas-reliefs of *Scenes from the Life of the Virgin* and which contains Bernardo Daddi's panel of the *Madonna delle Grazie* (1347).

▲ *Panorama of Piazza della Signoria.*

I n Roman times, the area that is now the civic centre of the town was occupied by dwelling houses and the theatre. At the end of the 13th century, the area was included in the town-planning scheme directed by Arnolfo di Cambio, who requisitioned and pulled down the houses of Ghibelline families standing there and began to build Palazzo Vecchio. Henceforward the piazza became the setting

Neptune Fountain

Bartolomeo Ammannati was architect to Grand Duke Cosimo I. He contributed to restructuring Palazzo Pitti, rebuilding the Carraia and Santa Trinita bridges and he worked on numerous mansions all over Florence; as a sculptor, his most important work is this fountain in the piazza, commissioned by Cosimo and sculpted between 1563 and 1575. In the centre of the polygonal basin is the large figure of *Neptune* (whose bearded features recall the artist's patron, Cosimo), standing on a coach drawn by sea-horses; all round the edge of the basin, the magnificent bronze figures of *Naiads, Tritons* and *Satyrs* reveal the hand of Giambologna, Ammannati's assistant.

On the steps of the Palace are placed: the *Marzocco*, the lion of the Florentine republic, a copy of Donatello's original, now in the Bargello; a copy of Michelangelo's *David*, now in the Academy, placed here in 1504 to personify the freedom that Florence yearned for in the brief republican period of those years; *Hercules and Cacus* by Bandinelli (1534) and two statuettes (perhaps *Philemon and Bausis* changed into plants) by De' Rossi and Bandinelli. On the left of the fountain is an imposing **equestrian monument to Cosimo I de' Medici** by Giambologna (1594). The reliefs around the base represent: the *Tuscan Senate Conferring the Title of Grand Duke on Cosimo I* (1537), *Pius V Presenting Cosimo with the Insignia of the Rank of Grand Duke* (1569), and *Cosimo Victoriously Entering Siena* (1557).

for public speeches, ceremonies, meetings, uproars, executions: famous, especially, that of *Girolamo Savonarola*, the preacher who was, for a short time, the arbiter of political life in the city and was excommunicated and burnt at the stake as a heretic on 23rd May 1498, on the spot now indicated by a plaque in front of the Neptune Fountain. The Gothic Loggia was built in the 14th century. Opposite the latter, at N° 5, is the **Alberto della Ragione Collection** (works of modern Italian art) and at N° 7 is **Palazzo Uguccioni**, built to a design by Michelangelo or Raphael, and on the east side the **Mercantile Tribunal**, built in 1359.

▲ ▶ The bronze equestrian monument to Cosimo I dei Medici, by Giambologna and the Neptune Fountain, by Bartolomeo Ammannati.

▲ ▶ *The Loggia dei Lanzi today* and *in an old painting.*

Loggia dei Lanzi

This is also called the Loggia della Signoria because it was built to shelter the public ceremonies of the Signoria, or even the Loggia dell'Orcagna from the name of the architect who, according to Vasari, designed it. The Lanzi were the Lanzichenecchi (Landsknechts), German mercenaries in the pay of Cosimo I, who used the Loggia as their bivouac for a certain period.

The Loggia was built between 1376 and 1383 by Benci di Cione and Simone Talenti. It consists of three large classical round arches, supported by composite piers and a spacious cross-vaulted porch. The lobed panels between the arches were carved between 1384 and 1389 upon designs by Agnolo Gaddi and enclose statues of the *Virtues*. Two heraldic *lions* flank the entrance: the one on the right is an ancient Roman statue, the other is 16th century. Under the right arch is the *Rape of the Sabine Women*, by Giambologna (1583), a work of refined virtuosity, which introduces the Baroque and was principally conceived to present and solve novel technical and compositional problems, wherefore it only received its name after it was finished. The left arch frames the *Perseus* by Benvenuto Cellini (1546-54): the hero holding up the head of Medusa has a stateliness worthy of Michelangelo and an almost Mannerist grace; the base is splendid, with statues and bas-reliefs that reveal the artist's skill as a goldsmith. The loggia also contains *Hercules and Nessus*, another group by Giambologna, *Menelaus Bearing the Body of Patroclus*, a Roman copy of a Greek original of the 4th century BC, six Roman female statues and the *Abduction of Polyxena*, a fine work by the nineteenth-century sculptor Pio Fedi.

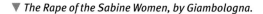
▼ *The Rape of the Sabine Women, by Giambologna.*

◀ *Perseus, by Benvenuto Cellini.*

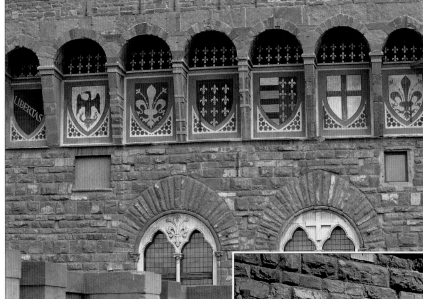

The civic coats of arms in the arches below the balustrade of Palazzo Vecchio's façade and *the entrance to the palace.*

bels, see (for instance) the Florentine symbol of red lily on white ground. Trap doors in the floor of the passage were used to drop stones, boiling oil or molten lead on assailants, in the case of uprisings or attacks on the palace. The tower, 94 metres high, masterfully placed off-centre, was finished in 1310. The palace was repeatedly enlarged, in 1343, in 1495 (by Cronaca) and in the 16th century by Vasari (who considerably altered the interior), by Giovanni Battista del Tasso and by Buontalenti.

Palazzo della Signoria, called Palazzo Vecchio (the old palace) after the middle of the 16th century when the Medici left it and moved to Palazzo Pitti, has always been the seat of the city's highest political authorities (the Municipal Council still has its offices in the palace) and a symbol of the strength of established institutions. The building was begun in 1299 and was probably designed by the great architect Arnolfo di Cambio. The original edifice is a massive rusticated cube, three storeys high, with great twin-mullioned windows on the two main floors and a battlemented, covered and projecting passage-way supported on corbels, above which rises the handsome, mighty tower. Nine *coats of arms*, symbolising the various regimes and rulers who have governed the Commune of Florence through the centuries, are repeated in the arches formed by the cor-

▲ *Palazzo Vecchio.*

▲ *The Putto, detail of Verrocchio's fountain.*

▲ *The Hall of the Five Hundred.*

The interior of the palace is of the greatest interest both architecturally and because of its contents. On the ground floor, the fine *Courtyard* by Michelozzo and the *Arms Hall* (entrance on the left side of the palace, used for temporary exhibitions); austere and bare, it is the only fourteenth-century room that has been left unaltered. On the first floor, the magnificent *Hall of the Five Hundred*, the *Hall of the Two Hundred*, by the brothers Da Maiano (1472-77), with a fine coffered ceiling in wood (this housed the Council of two hundred citizens who discussed wars and alliances, and is now used by the Borough Council); the *Apartments of Leo X*, with a chapel and rooms frescoed with *Scenes from the Lives of the Medicis* by Vasari and helpers (only the rooms of Leo X, Lorenzo the Magnificent and Cosimo I can be visited because the others are occupied by the Mayor and aldermen's offices).

On the second floor, the *Apartment of the Elements*, designed by Giovanni Battista del Tasso (c.1550). These rooms too were decorated

◄ *Hercules and Cacus, by Vincenzo de' Rossi.*

▲ *Pisa besieged and overthrown, by Giorgio Vasari*

by Vasari and helpers, some with fine inlaid cabinets. See also the lovely *Saturn Terrace* with its splendid view; the *Apartments of Eleonora of Toledo*, wife of Cosimo I, where special mention should be made of the *Gualdrada Room*, with another fine ebony cabinet inlaid with semiprecious stones, and the *Chapel*, entirely frescoed by Bronzino, who also painted the very fine altar-piece (*Pietà*, 1553); the *Chapel of the Signoria*, the very fine *Audience Hall*, with coffered ceiling and marble doorway, both by Benedetto da

◀ *Victory, by Michelangelo* and *Hercules and Diomedes, by Vincenzo de' Rossi.*

36

Maiano, which contains a beautiful wooden bench designed by Vasari; the magnificent **Lily Room** with Donatello's famous, dramatic bronze group of *Judith and Holophernes* (c. 1455), the **Map Room** and the **Chancery** next to it. Machiavelli, of whom there is a coloured clay bust and a portrait here, worked in this room for several years as the Secretary of the Republic; and here is the original of the charming fountain in the courtyard, *Cupid with a Dolphin*, by Verrocchio (1476).

On the mezzanine (reached from the Hall of the Elements) is a series of fifteen rooms containing an important collection of works of art recovered in Germany after World War II. See for instance: the *Crouching Aphrodite*, Roman sculpture, 2nd century AD; two fine coloured panels in opus sectile, 331 AD; Greek and Roman reliefs and sculptures of various epochs. Among the Medieval and later styles exemplified here, note: a beautiful little painting on wood of the *Madonna of Humility* attributed to Masolino and another very small one attributed to Masaccio; a large *Nativity* by Antoniazzo Romano; *Pygmalion and Galathea* by Bronzino; a fragment, barely roughhewn but very fine, of the *Rondanini Pietà* by Michelangelo; *Venus and Mercury Present their Son Anteros to Jove*, by Paolo Veronese; *Leda and the Swan*, by Tintoretto; *Portrait of Elizabeth of Valois*, by Coelho; *Judith with Holophernes' head* and a large *Equestrian Portrait of Giovanni Carlo Doria* by Rubens; a beautiful *Portrait of an Unknown Man* by Hans

▲ *Studiolo of Francesco I dei Medici.*

Memling; the *Ecstasy of St. Cecilia* by Bernardo Cavallino; an exquisite *Portrait of Felicita Sartori* by Rosalba Carriera; Venetian landscapes attributed to Francesco Guardi and the circle of Canaletto; and

a poignant *Maternity* by the nineteenth-century German painter Friedrich von Amerling. Also on the mezzanine are the **Museum of Musical Instruments**, containing rare and antique instruments of

The Lily Room.

various periods, and the **Loeser Collection**, an important legacy of sculptures and paintings by Tuscan artists from the 14th to the 16th centuries. The most important pieces are: in sculpture, two terracotta groups representing soldiers and knights, by Giovan Francesco Rustici (16th century); a splendid *Madonna and Child*, in painted wood, attributed to the school of Arnolfo di Cambio and a marble *Angel* by Tino da Camaino; in painting: the *Passion of Christ*, a curious work by Piero di Cosimo, end of 15th century: "an abstract and original spirit", Vasari called him in his Lives; a *Virgin and Child* by Pietro Lorenzetti (first half of 14th century) and the remarkable *Portrait of Laura Battiferri* (wife of the sculptor Ammannati) by Agnolo Bronzino.

A visit to the ***Tower*** is recommended in order to enjoy a stupendous, sweeping panorama over the city and its surroundings.

Judith and Holophernes, by Donatello.

▲ *The conquest of San Leo, by Giorgio Vasari.*

▼ *The Room of Jupiter.*

▲ *The Room of Caeres.*

UFFIZI GALLERY

The Uffizi is not only the oldest art gallery in the world, it is the most important in Italy and also one of the greatest in Europe and in the whole world, visited by more than a million people every year. The gallery owns about 4800 works, of which about 2000 are on view (1000 paintings, 300 sculptures, 46 tapestries, 14 pieces of furniture and pottery, besides 700 more paintings kept in the Vasari corridor), the rest are in storage or on loan to other museums. This enormous quantity of works includes countless masterpieces, some being among the highest achievements of Western art. The building containing the Gallery was built for Cosimo I in the

▲ *Cupid playing a lute, by Rosso Fiorentino.*

During his Florentine period this artist painted some of his most beautiful works. They are frank, lively, typically "local" blends of cultured and popular tradition. This pretty little Angel in the Tribuna was painted in Florence although the date is not certain (c. 1515-1522).

mid 16th century in the area between Palazzo Vecchio and the Arno to house the public offices (hence the name); the 11th century church of San Pier Scheraggio, and the old Mint, where the famous Florentine florins were coined, were partly incorporated.

The planning was entrusted to Giorgio Vasari (eminent and eclectic artistic figure of the time), who built

◀ *Piazzale degli Uffizi at night.*

▲ *The Uffizi loggia overlooking the Arno.*

it between 1559 and the year of his death (and that of Cosimo), 1574; the very original building consists of two long porticoes joined by a third side that abuts on the Arno with a magnificent arch of great scenic effect. The outside of the Uffizi is inspired by the style of Michelangelo's vestibule for the Laurentian Library: grey *pietra serena* architectural elements against gleaming white plaster. Together with the marvellous Corridor, it is undoubtedly Vasari's architectural masterpiece. Work on the Uffizi was resumed in 1580 by order of Francesco I and directed by Bernardo Buontalenti, who built the large Medici Theatre (dismantled in 1890) and the famous Tribuna; at the same time the loggia on the top storey was rebuilt, the offices were trans-

ferred elsewhere and some of the rooms were used for collections of arts items, arms, and scientific curiosities, and so the Gallery was born. The first nucleus of works already included paintings by Botticelli, Lippi and Paolo Uccello; about 1600, Ferdinando I had all the works at the Villa Medici in Rome transferred to the Uffizi; in 1631 Ferdinando II contributed with an important collection of paintings (originally in Urbino, the inheritance of his wife Vittoria della Rovere), including pieces by Piero della Francesca, Titian and Raphael; at the end of the 17th century, Cosimo III collected gems, medals and coins and brought the *Venus*, later known as the "Medici" Venus, and other important antique sculptures; Anna Maria Ludovica, Electress Palatine,

the last heir to the Medicis, enlarged the collection with Flemish and German paintings and left it in its entirety to the City of Florence in her will (1743). In the 19th century, after only part of the works of art stolen during the Napoleonic wars had been restored and after the creation of new specialised museums (Archaeological Museum, Bargello, Fra Angelico Museum, Museums of the Sciences, Silver Museum etc.) the Uffizi became what it is today. Extensive restoration of many of the works has been effected since the second world war, and is still in progress.

◄ Ognissanti Madonna, by Giotto (c. 1310).

This work originally hung in the Church of Ognissanti.
Even though the whole lacks the cohesive composition and dramatic force
of the fresco cycle, the Virgin has been rendered with a three-dimensionality
and severity of form hitherto unseen in 14th century painting.

▲ Rucellai Madonna, by Duccio di Buoninsegna (1285).

This superb altarpiece takes this name since
it was originally in the Rucellai Chapel
in the Church of Santa Maria Novella.
For years it was attributed to Cimabue,
whose influence, though superficial, is still evident.
Nevertheless, the weightless bodies, sinuous lines
and melancholy faces, Duccio's hallmarks,
leave no doubt as to the painter's identity.

*◄ Annunciation, by Simone Martini
and Lippo Memmi (1333).*

It originally hung in the Cathedral of Siena. The ethereal
figures caught in rhythmic poses and the decorative
details represent the epitome of refinement and charm:
the Sienese painter was actually the inititator
of the so-called International Gothic Style. The Saints
Ansano and Giulitta, on either side, are by Lippo Memmi.

► *Adoration of the Magi,*
by Gentile da Fabriano (*1423*).

Painted for the Strozzi Chapel in the Church of Santa Trinita, it is an exceptional example of Flamboyant Gothic style. The artist has given free rein to his lively imagination. The entourage of elaborately-costumed figures winds its way over hill and dale down to the lower lefthand corner where the Holy Family has been relegated. The whole composition gravitates towards the elegant figure of the youngest blond-haired Magus placed in the middle foreground.

▼ *Battle of San Romano,*
by Paolo Uccello (1456).

Probably painted for Cosimo the Elder, it is one of a set of three (the other two ended up in the Louvre and the London National Gallery in the 19th century). This large panel has a surprisingly "modern" look thanks to the abstract unreality of the colour and the foreshortening. This Tuscan artist was one of the first to study perspective.

◀ *Madonna and Child with two angels,*
by Filippo Lippi (c. 1464).

One of Lippi's late works, it is also one
of his most renowned. The key to this work,
originally in the Medici Villa at Poggio Imperiale,
is his masterful use of soft colours, which delicately
model the forms and the shimmering lights
that gilds both the foreground figures
and the airy landscapes in the background.

▼ *Portraits of Battista Sforza*
and *Federico da Montefeltro,*
by Piero della Francesca (c. 1465).

These portraits
of the Duke and Duchess of Urbino,
with allegories of their triumphs on the back,
were painted at the court of Urbino.
The landscapes reaching back behind
the figures are bathed in a clear glow
which makes the water and sky
appear almost transparent.

The group, also known as the "Doni Tondo" after the name of the patron, was painted when the artist was not yet thirty and reveals Michelangelo's predilection for sculpture, to which painting always had a secondary role.
The nudes in the background, perhaps influenced by Signorelli, are treated as if to simulate a monochrome bas-relief.

▶ Page 46: *Allegory of Spring, by Sandro Botticelli (1478).*

The name of this famous work was given by Vasari in the 16th century.
Painted for Lorenzo di Pierfrancesco dei Medici, this is acclaimed as one of Botticelli's masterpieces.
It is at the same time the most complete and perfect expression of his mature painting style and his ideal related to pure beauty.
The work alludes to the "reign of Venus" and the goddess is shown in the midst of a luxuriant garden of fruit and flowers.

▲ *Birth of Venus, by Sandro Botticelli (c. 1486).*

Commissioned by Lorenzo di Pierfrancesco dei Medici
this work represent Venus just as she is coming
to life, carried ashore by the concerted
huffing and puffing of the Zephyr winds.
An Hour of Spring waits
to cover her with a flowery cloak.

◀ *Baptism of Christ,
by Andrea del Verrocchio and Leonardo da Vinci.*

Verrocchio's paintings are sometimes a bit stiff,
maybe because he could not bear to rid his figures
of the metallic plasticity of his sculpture.
In this work, however, the harsh effect
is alleviated by the gentle brushstroke of his apprentice
Leonardo da Vinci, who added
a touch of delicate shading to the forms.

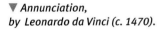 *Madonna of the Goldfinch,
by Raphael (1506).*

This painting was commissioned
by Vincenzo Nasi, a wealthy Florentine.
Leonardo's influence is clearly visible
in the pyramidal composition
and use of "sfumato", which here seems
to envelop the solid forms,
softening everything and creating
a delicate, luminous effect.

▼ *Annunciation,
by Leonardo da Vinci (c. 1470).*

This work was executed
for the Monastery of Monteoliveto
near Florence and came to the Uffizi
in 1870. One of Leonardo's earliest
paintings, it still follows the traditional
early 15th century compositional
scheme along a single picture plane
with a landscape in the background
shown in perspective.

◀ Madonna of the Harpies, by Andrea del Sarto (c. 1517).

Painted for the Convent of San Francesco in Florence, this work takes its name from the two harpies carved on the corners of the pedestal that supports the figure of the Virgin.
The monumental quality of the figures is clearly a result of Michelangelo's influence.

▼ Venus of Urbino, by Titian (1538).

Commissioned by Guidobaldo da Montefeltro, Duke of Urbino, it came into the Medici collection in the 17th century as part of Della Rovere testament. Titian's extraordinary technical skill is revealed in the warm flesh tones and glowing palette. A masterful touch is the placing of the two female figures in the background, to convey a feeling of realistic intimacy.

▲ *Still life with fruit, insects
and a lizard, by Rachel Ruysch.*

Born in Amsterdam, this artist
was one of the many painters
who chose to limit her production
to a specialised field that took
the name of "still life",
a practice frequently adopted
throughout the 17th century.

► *Portrait of the Countess
of Chinchon's mother on horseback,
by Francisco Goya.*

This is a splendid example
of the great Spaniard's skill in rendering
his sitters' psychological reality.
An unconventional figure,
Goya rejected the 18th century
art's academic canons and painted
according to his own ideas.
His delicate luminous palette
and painting style convey
great force and intensity.

◄ *Overall view of the Tribuna.*

▼ *Medici Venus (2nd century BC).*

◄ *The 17th century octagonal table, by Jacopo Ligozzi and Poccetti.*

▲ *Study of a man's head, by Michelangelo.*

The rooms are on the first floor of the Uffizi in the place of the former Medici Theatre, built by Buontalenti in 1585 for court festivities, balls and plays, and are reached by going up the magnificent staircase designed by Vasari. The large theatre, the first of the modern epoch, occupied most of this wing of the building and saw the birth of Melodramma (early 17th century). Application must be made to visit the Drawing and Print rooms which are only accessible to students: the first room is used for temporary exhibitions.

Vasari Corridor

Conceived as a passage by air from the Grand Ducal Palace, Pitti, to the seat of government (the Uffizi), and, along another short passage, to Palazzo Vecchio, this singular feat of architecture and town planning was executed in the short space of five months, in 1565, by Giorgio Vasari, commissioned by Cosimo I.

▼ *Self-portrait, by Giorgio Vasari.*

The drawings and prints collection

This collection of drawings and prints, now one of the greatest in the world, was begun by Cardinal Leopoldo dei Medici in the 17th century; when he died (1675) the material was brought from Palazzo Pitti to the Uffizi and was rearranged by Filippo Baldinucci, a scholar commissioned to do this by Cosimo III; it already amounted to about 100 volumes. The collection was then increased by legacies and purchases, and today reaches the considerable figure of more than 50,000 drawings and 60,000 prints by all the major Italian and foreign artists (only a few of them modern); these include Paolo Uccello, Fra Angelico, Botticelli, Leonardo, Michelangelo, Raphael, Brueghel, Dürer, Lorrain and countless other.

The Vasari Corridor starts from the Uffizi on the third floor between Room XXV and Room XXXIV, runs along the Arno over an arcade, crosses the river over Ponte Vecchio, passes between houses and palaces on the other side of the river, along beside the façade of the curch of Santa Felicita (the Grund Dukes attended religious services there, unseen in a private box); it continues along the side of Boboli Garden and, after a distance of nearly a kilometre, enters the Palazzo Pitti. It was damaged in World War II and only reopened in 1973.

About seven hundred paintings are on view, including seventeenth and eighteenth century Italian works, potraits of the Medicis and the Lor-

▶ *Self-portrait, by Diego Velazquez.*

raines, and above all the famous collection of self-portraits, the most complete in the world, extending from the fourteenth century to the present time, including nearly all the greater Italian artists and numerous foreign ones.

◀ *Boy removing a thorn from his foot, Roman copy after a hellenistic original (2ⁿᵈ-1ˢᵗ century BC).*

PONTE VECCHIO

As the name implies, it is the oldest bridge in Florence: it has, in fact, existed since the time of the Roman colony, when the piers were of stone and the roadway of wood; destroyed by flooding in 1117, it was completely rebuilt in stone but collapsed again in the terrible flood of 4th November 1333. It was rebuilt for the last time in 1345 (perhaps by the architect-cum-painter Taddeo Gaddi) with three spans, very wide, planned with room for shops on either side. First of all the butchers settled

▼ *View of Ponte Vecchio from Borgo San Jacopo.*

▲ ◄ *Ponte Vecchio seen from the second corridor of the Uffizi Gallery and the Bust of Benvenuto Cellini, by Romanelli.*

there (but later also grocers, smiths, shoemakers, etc.); these built the typical shops with their back rooms projecting over the river, resting on supports and brackets.

In 1591 Ferdinando I evicted them all, only allowing the shops to the goldsmiths; and since then the bridge has been like two long jewellery-shop windows, only interrupted by the two clearings in the middle, the one looking downstream has a *Bust of Benvenuto Cellini*, "master of the goldsmiths" by Raffaello Romanelli (1900).

On November 4th 1966 the latest, dramatic flooding of Florence put the bridge to the test again: the structure itself stood up well, but the fury of the waters burst through the gold-smiths' shops at the back and swept away quantities of jewels.

PALAZZO PITTI

▲ ▶ *Palazzo Pitti* and
the majestic inner courtyard, by Ammannati.

By the middle of the 15th century, power was practically in the hands of the Medici family. Cosimo the Elder governed Florence from his new palace in Via Larga. Luca Pitti, however, his erstwhile friend, now led the faction that was most hostile to him and to his son Piero.

Luca, wanted a palace finer than the one that Michelozzo was building for the Medicis. He chose the site on the hill of Boboli and commissioned Brunelleschi to design a building with windows as large as the doorways of the Medici palace and so large, that the Medici palace would fit into his courtyard. Brunelleschi accepted with alacrity (Cosimo had previously rejected his plan for Via Larga) and produced the plans about 1445. Work began in 1457 (after the master's death) under the direction of Luca Fancelli, Brunelleschi's pupil.

The façade overlooking the piazza consisted only of the seven central windows; it was on three storeys separated by slender balconies and covered with rusticated stone. At the death of Luca Pitti in 1473 the palace was still incomplete; then

▲ *The Iliad Room and the statue of Charity, by Lorenzo Bartolini.*

the Pitti family fell into disfavour, and Eleonora of Toledo, the wife of Cosimo I, bought the building and the land behind it in 1549. In the 16th and 17th century this became the palace of the Medici, who enlarged it, created a garden on the Boboli hill, lengthened the building to nine windows each side, employing Giulio and Alfonso Parigi, and decorated the interior sumptuously. In the 18th century Ruggieri and Poccianti built the two porticoed side wings that enclose the piazza (the so-called "rondò").

The remarkable fact is that each successive enlargement substantially respected the original design by Brunelleschi, both in form and material. During the period in which Florence was the capital of Italy (1865-71) the palace was the residence of Vittorio Emanuele II. Since 1919 it has been the property of the Italian State, together with its magnificent collections formed in centuries of devotion to art.

There are seven museums here: the **Palatine Gallery**, the **Monumental Apartments**, the **Silver Museum**, the **Gallery of Modern Art**, the **Costume Gallery**, the **Coach Museum** and the **Porcelain Museum**.

◄ *Woman's gown of Italian make, 1840-45 (Costume Gallery).*

PALATINE GALLERY

The Palatine Gallery has its own particular character: it is not an organic collection systematically arranged to present a "comprehensive review" of the art of a certain period or periods (like the Uffizi); it is, rather, a typical 17th century picture gallery that reflects the taste of its creator and hence of contemporary fashion; even the arrangement of the pictures manifests a decorative intention alien to the museographical criteria of today. This is, in fact, the charm of the Palatine Gallery, a "private" museum, almost a home, with its elegant furniture, ornaments, ebony cabinets, inlaid tables, stuccoes, tapestries and fine cornices.

The idea of this collection goes back to two of the last Medicis, Cosimo II and Ferdinando II, who commissioned a great Baroque decorator, Pietro da Cortona, to fresco some of the rooms on the first floor of the Palazzo Pitti with allegorical mythological subjects celebrating the glories of the house of Medici (1641-47); he began to arrange pictures in the rooms, creating a new family collection to complement that already existing in the Uffizi. The Lorraines continued both with the decoration of the rooms and the collection of works of art; in 1828 Grand Duke Pietro Leopoldo opened the museum to the public, a liberal gesture quite in the spirit of the new European tendency towards a greater diffusion of culture.

▲ *Madonna of the Chair, by Raphael (c. 1513).*

This much copied work was the first painting to be requisitioned by Napoleon's commissars in 1799 for transferring to the Louvre. In 1598 it was brought in the Uffizi Tribune and endly moved to the Palazzo Pitti. This is one of Raphael's most universally acclaimed masterpieces. The painting's elegance lead critics to believe that it was done for a private customer, perhaps Pope Leo X.

Limited at first to the fine *Rooms of Venus, Apollo, Mars, Jupiter* and *Saturn*, the collection grew to its present dimensions until 1928, when a great number of paintings were exchanged with the Uffizi and many 16th and 17th century works were acquired.

◀ *The Venus Room with Antonio Canova's Venus Italicus in the centre.*

In the 17th century it belonged to Cardinal Carlo de' Medici and was later added to Cosimo III's collection. It was painted during the years Raphael spent in Florence and it depicts a local noblewoman resting on her abdomen, almost symbolic of pregnancy, hence the name. The influence of Leonardo da Vinci was fundamental in this period, as we can see from the arrangement of the composition and the volumetric play created by his great mastery of colour.

▲ *Madonna of the Grand Duke, by Raphael (1506).*

One of Raphael's masterpieces and the oldest, it got its name from the fact that the Grand Duke Ferdinand III purchased it in Florence in 1799, during his exile in Vienna. It was painted when the artist absorbed much of Leonardo's art, as can be seen from the composition and the incomparable sweetness in the embrace between mother and child, enhanced by the dark background.

▶ *Portrait of a Lady or "The Beautiful Simonetta", by Sandro Botticelli (end of 15th cent.).*

Simonetta Vespucci was the woman loved by Giuliano dei Medici, Lorenzo the Magnificent's brother. She died very young and Pulci sang her in his work "Stanze". The painting has also been attributed to Ghirlandaio.

▲ *Portrait of a Woman or "La Velata", by Raphael (1516).*

This work came to the Palazzo Pitti in 1621 as part of the Marquis Matteo Botti's bequest.
The woman depicted, according to Vasari accounts has been identified with Margherita, known as "La Fornarina",
daughter of Francesco Luti of Siena and said to have been Raphael's mistress.
The rich gowns, soft and somptuous, and mainly the veil and the hand over her heart would indicate a married woman.

◀ *Portrait of a Man or The Man with the Grey Eyes,*
by Titian (c. 1540-1545).

It depicts an unknown man painted in an informal
and modern pose. The arm casually by his side
and his penetrating gaze reveal nobility and charm of his personality.
The monumental image, with its severe greys and blacks,
is enlivened by the flesh tones and white lace on the collar and cuffs.

▲ *Portrait of a Lady or "La Bella" by Titian*

This portrait was dubbed with this title when
at the end of the 18th century, in an attempt to identify the model,
a certain resemblance to the "Venere di Urbino" was noted.
It was mentioned for the first time in a letter dated 1536
from Francesco Maria, Duke of Urbino, to Titian.
The work, depicting a woman with her charming face
and beautiful blue brocade dress, came to Florence along
with the bequest of the Grand Duchess Vittoria della Rovere (1631).

◀ *Magdalene, by Perugino (1500).*

▲ *Magdalene, by Titian (1531).*

Painted for Guidobaldo, Duke of Urbino, this is one of the artist's most famous work.
It was brought to Florence with the bequest of Vittoria della Rovere. In the warm tones of the flesh
and the brilliant auburn of the mass of hair, Titian's sense of colour finds here one of its finest expression.
This painting of incomparable value is both a prototype of religious devotion and filled with the ambiguity of much Baroque art.

◀ The Four Philosophers,
by Pieter Paul Rubens (c. 1611).

This great work reveals the influence of Titian's
and Tintoretto's Venetian style on Flemish art.
The painting depicts, starting from the right,
Rubens himself, his brother Philip
and the humanists Justus Lipsius
and Jan Van de Wouwère; in the background
we can see the ruins of the Palatine Hill
and the Church of Saint Theodore in Rome.

▼ The Consequences of War,
by Pieter Paul Rubens.

It was ordered by Justus Sustermans,
the Flemish painter who lived in Florence in 1637.
The painting arrived in 1638 and was transferred
to the Palazzo Pitti in 1691 when Ferdinando dei Medici
purchased it from the deceased painter's heirs.
Rubens' anguish over the difficult situation in Flanders
comes through in the work's bloody scene.
The tragic violence of the subject is matched
by excited and rhytmic tones and it is all emphasized
by bright colors that contrast with Venus'pale skin.

▲ The Throne Room.

▲ The Dining Room.

Monumental Apartments

This is the name given to a series of richly decorated rooms on the first floor, formerly the residence of the rulers of the houses of Medici, Lorraine and Savoy. As a matter of fact the only ones who lived there permanently were the Medicis, from Cosimo I to Gian Gastone (died 1737) who used to stay in bed the whole time, governing the state, eating, or receiving

▲ *The Queen's Room.*

guests or mistresses. He was succeeded by his sister Anna Maria Ludovica, who left the Gran Duchy to the Lorraine family. The Lorraines preferred to live in the Villa of Poggio Imperiale, while the Savoy family had a liking for the Villa della Petraia, at Castello.

The most interesting rooms are: the *Green Room* with 18th century Gobelin tapestries and a large 17th century cabinet; the *Throne Room*; the *Chapel*; the *Parrot Room*, the first of those forming the Apartments of Queen Margherita; the *Yellow Room*; the *Queen's Room* with oriental style decorations; the *Apartment of Umberto I* with fine portraits and furnishings; the *Bona Room* with frescoes by Poccetti, and the neoclassical *White Room*, the large and luminous palace ballroom, where temporary exhibitions are now frequently held.

▶ *Pendant with a Rooster, German goldsmith's work in the Silver Museum (16th cent.).*

Silver Museum

It was instituted in 1919 and arranged on the ground floor of Palazzo Pitti, in the rooms that were used as the summer apartments of the Grand Dukes. Among the most interesting of these, from the point of view of decoration, are the **Room of Giovanni da San Giovanni** and the three successive ones, frescoed by Colonna and Mitelli between 1638 and 1644.

The prestigious collection includes goldsmiths' work, enamels, cameos, crystal and carved or inlaid semi-precious stone objects, acquired by the Medicis and the Hapsburgs. Among the most important pieces are: semi-precious stone vases belonging to Lorenzo the Magnificent; 17th century German ivories; a *vase in lapis lazuli* by Buontalenti (1583): the jewels of the bishop-princes of Salzburg; a *drinking cup belonging to Diane de Poitiers* (16th century); a relief in gold, enamel and semi-precious stones of *Cosimo II in Prayer* (17th century).

▲ *Portrait of the Daughter of Jack La Bolina, by Vittorio Corcos.*

◀ *Singing a stornello, by Silvestro Lega (1867).*

Gallery of Modern Art

This contains a representative collection of 19th century painting, especially Tuscan. The first group of rooms is devoted to neoclassical and romantic works: a *Head of Calliope* by Canova; *Hercules at the crossroads* by Pompeo Batoni, the *Battle of Legnano* by Cassioli, works by Benvenuti, Duprè and Bezzuoli. In the second group are paintings of the second half of the century, with particular emphasis on the Macchiaioli, the most important current in Italian art at the time; the *Man caught by the stirrup*, the *Cavalry Charge* and the *Palmieri Rotunda* by Giovanni Fattori; works by Lega, Corcos and Signorini, and lastly paintings by Elisabeth Chaplin, Previati, Medardo Rosso and Vermehren.

◀ *Bacchus Fountain, by Valerio Cioli.*

▲ *The complex of the Boboli Gardens with the Kaffeehaus.*

The creation of a garden on the hill at Boboli began at the same time as the rebuilding of the Palazzo Pitti for Cosimo I and Eleonora of Toledo at about the middle of the 16th century. The architect and sculptor Niccolò Pericoli, called "Tribolo", was given the task of designing a garden in accordance with the new Renaissance mode which exacted more stately proportions than the Medieval private "viridarium" (or greenery) had accustomed people to. The Renaissance garden was the symbol of the Prince's power, the scene of parties and plays, a place of relaxation for the court, where one could wander through groves populated by allegorical statues, grottoes and fountains. Boboli underwent many alterations owing to variations in taste, but the design remained substantially the same.

Near the entrance is the curious *Bacchus Fountain* in which Valerio Cioli portrayed a dwarf of the court of Cosimo I astride a tortoise. Further on is the *Grotta del Buontalenti*, built between 1583 and 1588 for the eccentric Francesco I; the

◀ *Entrance to the Fountain of the Ocean, by Giambologna.*

▲ *Grotta del Buontalenti.*

first chamber is like a real cave decorated with sculptured forms that look like animals. In the corners are four copies of Michelangelo's *Prisoners* (Accademia Gallery) – the originals used to stand here. In the cave behind, the group of *Paris and Helena*, by Vincenzo de' Rossi. Last comes a small grotto with a *Venus* by Giambologna.

Going on, one comes to the *Amphitheatre*, first made in grass in the 16th century and remade in the 18th, for the performance of plays. The Egyptian obelisk in the centre was brought to Rome from Luxor in the Imperial epoch. Going up to the left one comes to the *Neptune Fishpond* and the *Giardino del Cavaliere*, where stands the **Porcelain Museum**. Walking straight on, along a wide *avenue*, one reaches the beautiful *Piazzale dell'Isolotto*, with its large pool and island, planted with lemon trees, and the *Fountain of the Ocean* by Giambologna. The garden is full of other antique and Renaissance statues.

▲ *The so-called "Viottolone", flanked by statues.*

69

SANTA MARIA DEL CARMINE

With Santo Spirito, this is the most important church on the south side of the Arno. It was founded in 1268 by the Carmelite Friars. In 1771 it was burnt down, except for the Corsini and Brancacci chapels and the sacristy; however, the parts destroyed were completely rebuilt a few years later. The unfinished façade is a high, severe wall of rough stone.

The interior is prevalently 18th century. The *Corsini Chapel*, at the end of the left transept, by Silvani and Foggini, with ceiling frescoed by Luca Giordano with the *Apotheosis of St. Andrea Corsini* (1682), is a 17th century masterpiece.

At the end of the opposite transept is the main feature of the church: the *Brancacci Chapel*, whose decoration is a milestone in Western art history. The murals were commissioned in 1425 by Felice Brancacci, a rich Florentine merchant and diplomat to the painter Masolino da Panicale, who still conformed to the Gothic taste, but was also

▲ *The Brancacci Chapel.*

▼ *The façade of Santa Maria del Carmine.*

open to the new ideas that were beginning to emerge in Tuscan painting at the time. The pioneer and great master of this renewal was the colleague Masolino chose to work with on the Brancacci Chapel: Masaccio. The latter probably replaced the older painter in the following year, when Masolino was called to the court of Hungary, but for reasons unknown (perhaps his extreme poverty obliged him to leave the city), he did not finish the work, which was instead completed by Filippino Lippi between 1481 and 1485. The best work of Masaccio's brief career (he died in 1428 at the age of 27) is in the Brancacci Chapel: his frescoes won the unconditioned admiration of Verrocchio, Fra Angelico, Leonardo, Botticelli, Perugino, Michelangelo and Raphael; his startling rediscovery of the classical laws of perspective which, for the first time in Italian painting, endows his figures with an almost sculptural solidity, the dramatically essential way in which he relates the episodes of the New and Old Testaments, recalls the superb simplicity of Giotto, but also make him the first great master of

► *Expulsion from Paradise, by Masaccio, detail of the left wall.*

the Italian Renaissance. The cycles of illustrations on the walls of the Brancacci Chapel are two: *Original Sin* and *Scenes from the Life of St. Peter;* among the most significant are the *Expulsion from Paradise*, a powerful masterpiece by Masaccio which faces the quite different dramatic tension in the *Temptation of Adam and Eve* by Masolino, on the wall opposite; *St. Peter Heals a Cripple and Restores Tabitha to Life*, by both artists; *St. Peter baptising the Neophytes* and *The Tribute Money*, both by Masaccio.

▼ *View of the right wall of the Brancacci Chapel.*

The church of Santo Spirito stands on the northern side of the square. The original plan, by Filippo Brunelleschi (1444), was for a church facing in the opposite direction, towards the Arno, overlooking a large piazza; but it could not be carried out owing to the opposition of the landowners involved. After Brunelleschi's death, his design was largely respected by Antonio Manetti and other pupils as regards the interior, while the simple façade is 17th century. The slender bell tower was built by Baccio d'Agnolo at the beginning of the 16th century.

The spacious and solemn interior recalls the symmetry and rhythmical perfection achieved by Bru-

▲ *The façade* and *the interior of the Church of Santo Spirito.*

◀ *Virgin and Child with Saints and the Commissioners* or *Nerli Altarpiece*, by Filippino Lippi (c. 1490).

tyrs by Alessandro Allori (1574). In the predella is a view of the original façade of *Palazzo Pitti*. In the left transept is the **Corbinelli Chapel**, an elegant piece of architecture and sculpture by Andrea Sansovino (1492). Next to it is the *Holy Trinity with SS. Catherine and Magdalene* attributed to Francesco Granacci.

Off the left aisle is an elegant vestibule by Cronaca (1494) with a fine barrel vault. This leads into the beautiful octagonal *Sacristy*, with dome, by Giuliano da Sangallo (1492). Leaving the church, on the right is the entrance to the **Cenacolo**, the refectory of the Augustinian monastery that used to exist here. The wall at the end of the room is covered with a large fresco by Andrea Orcagna (c. 1360) representing two scenes, one above the other: a wonderful *Crucifixion* and a *Last Supper*.

nelleschi in San Lorenzo, except for the variation of a dome above the presbytery and the continuation of the side aisles in the transept and the apse. The elaborate Baroque high altar by Giovanni Caccini (1608) stands in the centre of the presbytery. In the right transept is a fine *Virgin and Child with Saints and the Commissioners* by Filippino Lippi (c. 1490) with an interesting view of Florence in the background. In the apse is a polyptych by Maso di Banco representing the *Virgin and Child with Saints*; on a nearby altar is a painting of the *Holy Mar-*

SAN FREDIANO IN CESTELLO

T he church was designed by Antonio Ferri, as the elegant dome (1698); the fine Baroque interior contains, among other works, the exquisite *Smiling Madonna*, a coloured wooden statue of the Pisan school, 13th century.

▶ *The Church of San Frediano in Cestello.*

PONTE SANTA TRINITA

After Ponte Vecchio, this is certainly the finest and noblest in the city. Built in 1252 and rebuilt several times, it has now the form given by Bartolomeo Ammannati in 1567-70. At the ends are four statues of the *Seasons*, 1608. The most famous of these is the one representing *Spring*, by Pietro Francavilla (at the corner with Lungarno Acciaioli).

▼ ▶ *Ponte Santa Trinita*
and *two of the statues that decorate*
each of the four corner plinths of the bridge:
Winter, by Taddeo Landini
and *Autumn, by Giovan Battista Caccini.*

PIAZZA SANTA TRINITA

▲ ▶ *The Statue of Justice on the column standing in Piazza Santa Trinita and Via Tornabuoni in a 19th century painting.*

Surrounded by noble mansions, the piazza is at the beginning of Via Tornabuoni, with the **Column of Justice** in the centre. This came from the Baths of Caracalla in Rome and supports the *Statue of Justice* by Francesco del Tadda (1581).

▶ *Francesco Sassetti,
detail of the Sassetti Chapel frescoed by Domenico Ghirlandaio.*

The fine large battlemented palace that extends as far as Lungarno Acciaioli is the 13th century **Palazzo Spini-Ferroni** (restored in the 19th century); at No. 1 of the piazza is **Palazzo Bartolini-Salimbeni,** Baccio d'Agnolo's masterpiece, with its unusual stone-cross partitioned windows (1520-23).

The **Church of Santa Trinita** goes back to the 11th century; the Mannerist façade is by Buontalenti (1593-94); the interior is very rich in works of art, that include: a frescoed chapel (fourth on the right) with a painting on wood by Lorenzo Monaco (1420-25); a *Magdalen* in wood by Desiderio da Settignano (1464; fifth

chapel on the left); the famous *Sassetti Chapel* frescoed by Domenico Ghirlandaio with scenes from the life of St. Francis (right transept); the *Tomb of Benozzo Federighi*, a masterpiece by Luca della Robbia (c. 1450, left transept), and in the Sacristy, the Renaissance *Tomb of Onofrio Strozzi*, by Piero di Niccolò Lamberti.

▼ *The Adoration of the Shepherds, by Domenico Ghirlandaio.*

▲ *The Church of Santa Trinita.*

PALAZZO STROZZI

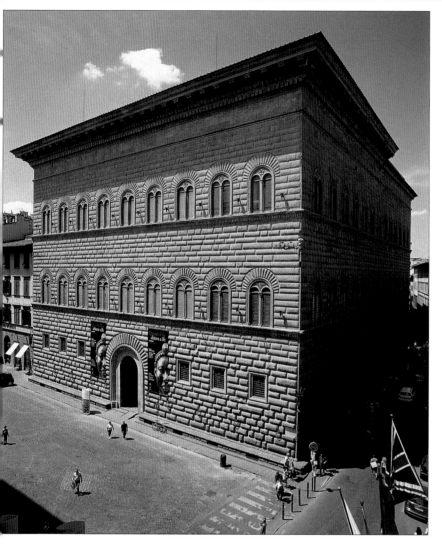

Filippo Strozzi, a Florentine merchant of long-standing wealth (he had the merit of introducing into Tuscany not only the cultivation of artichokes, but also a good variety of fig), commissioned Benedetto da Maiano to build the palace in 1489; Benedetto was succeeded by Cronaca who directed the work until 1504. Later the construction was interrupted and resumed several times; the Strozzi family fell into disfavour in 1538, the palace was confiscated by Cosimo I dei Medici and given back thirty years later. Now it houses cultural organisations and exhibitions. The massive building (by many considered the finest Renaissance building) has a stone plinth all round it at the base, projecting like a bench; the exterior recalls that of Palazzo Medici-Riccardi, with pronounced rustication; at the top is a magnificent *cornice* by Cronaca; the two upper storeys have fine mullioned, twin-arched windows; there is a majestic porticoed **Courtyard** inside, also by Cronaca.

◄ *Palazzo Strozzi.*

OGNISSANTI

The 13th century church of Ognissanti (All Saints) stands in the piazza of the same name overlooking the Arno. It was completely remade in the 17th century. The pleasing Baroque façade is by Matteo Nigetti (1637); the bell-tower is older (14th century). Inside are several paintings on wood and frescoes of the 15th-16th century, including the *Madonna of Mercy,* by Ghirlandaio, commissioned by the Vespucci family (the future great navigator Amerigo also appears in it; 1472). Beside the church is the *Refectory,* with the famous *Last Supper* by Ghirlandaio; there are also two detached frescoes, formerly in the church: *St. Jerome in his Study,* also by Ghirlandaio, and *St. Augustine in his Study* by Botticelli.

► *Saint Jerome in his Study, by Domenico Ghirlandaio.*

Santa Maria Novella

The building, begun in 1221, was designed by the architect friars Fra Sisto and Fra Ristoro. The lower part of the façade, first erected in 1300, was completed in the typical Florentine Romanesque-Gothic style before the middle of the 14th century. After the middle of the 15th century, Leon Battista Alberti, the great theorist of architecture, finished off the inlaid marble façade by adding the central doorway and the upper part, of extraordinary elegance, with a rose window, tympanum and side scrolls.

The Cistercian Gothic interior, in the "softened" form that this style took in Italy, is in the shape of a Latin cross, with nave and side aisles and composite columns. An in-

credible number of art works decorate the walls and chapels. In the second bay of the right aisle is the *Tomb of the Beata Villana*, by Bernardo Rossellino (1451). The right transept leads to the **Rucellai Chapel**; on the altar is a *Madonna* by Nino Pisano, in the floor the *Tomb-stone of Leonardo Dati*, by Ghiberti (1425). The **Filippo Strozzi Chapel** to the right of the high altar is covered with frescoes by Filippino Lippi (c. 1500) with *Stories of SS. Philip and John the Evangelist*. The **Chancel** was frescoed by Domenico Ghirlandaio (c. 1495, young Michelangelo was probably one of his

◄ *The Crowning of the Virgin: stained glass rose-window, designed by Andrea di Bonaiuto.*

◄ ▲ *The façade* and *the interior of Santa Maria Novella.*

▲ *The Holy Trinity, by Masaccio.*

▲ *The Apparition of the Angel to Zacharias, by Domenico Ghirlandaio.*

▲ *The Birth of the Virgin, by Domenico Ghirlandaio.*

assistants) with beautiful *Scenes of the Life of the Virgin*. The **Gondi Chapel** (left of the chancel) has the celebrated *Crucifix* by Brunelleschi. In the **Strozzi Chapel** (left transept) are frescoes by Nardo di Cione (c. 1367; a remarkable representation of *Hell*). In the **Sacristy** nearby is a *Crucifix*, a youthful work by Giotto. Lastly, at the third bay of the left aisle, the marvellous *Holy Trinity* by Masaccio (c. 1427) and the *Pulpit* designed by Filippo Brunelleschi.

Outside, to the right, is the interesting group of cloisters. The fourteenth-century **Green Cloister** has frescoes in the lunettes by fifteenth-century painters including Paolo Uccello, who painted the *Scenes from Genesis* (a very fine *Flood*, c. 1430). The **Spanish Chapel** is off the cloister, frescoed in the 14th century by Andrea di Bonaiuto, and used in the 16th century by Eleonora of Toledo's Spanish courtiers. Close by, in the **Chiostrino dei Morti**, a fourteenth century window with the *Crowning of the Virgin* closes the façade oculus.

▼ *The Church militant and triumphant, detail of the Spanish Chapel, frescoed by Andrea di Bonaiuto and assistants.*

▲ *Façade* and *interior*
of the Church of San Lorenzo.

An ancient basilica, consecrated in 393 by St. Ambrose, bishop of Milan, it was probably the first church to be built on Florentine ground. Rebuilt in the 11th century, it was radically restored in the 15th century for the Medicis, for whom it was the family church.

The interior, spacious, light and elegant, is an early Florentine Renaissance masterpiece; it was designed by Brunelleschi in 1420 and he directed the work from 1442 until his death in 1446. It is in the form of a Latin cross and has a nave and two aisles with side chapels. There are numerous masterpieces, in-cluding two bronze *Pulpits* by Donatello at the end of the nave, the master's last work (about 1460), completed after his death by pupils; a fine marble *Tabernacle* by Desiderio da Settignano (mid 15th century) opposite the pulpit on the right; the *Marriage of the Virgin*, a painting by Rosso Fiorentino (1523) in the second chapel on the right; a remarkable *Annunciation*, with *Scenes of the life of St. Nicholas of Bari* by Filippo Lippi (c. 1440) in the predella, in the left chapel of the left transept; also a large fresco representing the *Martyrdom of St. Laurence* by Bronzino (1565-69) in the left aisle opposite the pulpit.

Finally, the **Old Sacristy**, exceptionally important for its architecture and works of art, is off the left transept. Elegant and of crystalline

simplicity in its spatial conception, it fully expresses Brunelleschi's architectural ideal (1420-29). The eight fine tondi in the lunettes and pendentives (four with *Scenes from the Life of St. John the Evangelist* and four with the *Evangelists*) are by Donatello, as are the two bronze doors beside the altar and a fine clay *Bust of St. Laurence*; in the centre of the chapel, under a large marble table, is the *Tomb of Giovanni di Bicci dei Medici* and *Piccarda Bueri*, the parents of Cosimo the Elder, by Andrea Cavalcanti (1434); on the left wall, under a large arch, is the *Tomb of Piero the Gouty* and *Giovanni dei Medici*, sons of Cosimo the Elder, by Andrea del Verrocchio, helped probably by the youthful Leonardo (1472).

Laurentian Library

This library was founded by Cosimo the Elder and enlarged by Lorenzo the Magnificent; the entrance is in the beautiful cloister of San Lorenzo.
It is extraordinarily rich in old manuscripts and codices. Among the most important are the so-called *Medici Virgil* (4th-5th century), the *Pandects of Justinian* (6th century), the oldest existing examples of the *tragedies of Aeschylus* (11th century) and of the writing of *Thucydides, Herodotus* and *Tacitus* (10th century). Michelangelo began the building in 1524 and designed the *Entrance Hall* and the large, elegant *Reading Room*, while the *Vestibule* was completed by Vasari and other architects.

MEDICI CHAPELS

The shrine and mausoleum of the Medicis, by the church of San Lorenzo (the entrance is at the back of the church in Piazza Madonna degli Aldobran-dini), the Medici chapels are an important architectural and artistic complex, famous above all for the statues by Michelangelo. The Princes' Chapel is also impressive on the outside: its structure resembles that of the dome of the Cathedral, octagonal in form with small apses. Inside there is first a wide crypt, which leads to the sumptous *Princes' Chapel*, ordered by Ferdinando I in 1602. Work began two years later upon a plan by Matteo Nigetti, and Buontalenti, and continued for more than a century. The great octagonal space is lined with inlaid semi-precious stone wall panels of spectacular effect. Against the walls are the *sarcophagi* of six Medici grand dukes; above those of Ferdinando I and Cosimo II, statues in gilt bronze by Ferdinando Tacca;

◀▼ *The dome of the Princes' Chapel* and *its majestic interior.*

▲ *The dome's frescoed vault of the Prices' Chapel.*

below: the sixteen *coats of arms* of Tuscan cities, in inlaid semi-precious stones. The chapel dome is frescoed with *Scenes from the Old and New Testaments*, by Pietro Benvenuti (1828).

A corridor leads to the **New Sacristy**, the famous and beautiful chapel built by Michelangelo for Cardinal Giulio de' Medici, later Pope Clement VII. Michelangelo worked on it, through various vicissitudes, from 1520 until he departed from Florence (1534), leaving it unfinished. On a square plan, with its grey sandstone (*pietra serena*) on white plaster, the chapel resembles the structure of Brunelleschi's Old Sacristy, but with much richer and more complex architectural decoration (niches, windows, arches etc.). Out of the many tombs intended, the only

▶ *The coat of arms of Florence.*

statue did not resemble the deceased man at all, Michelangelo was supposed to have retorted that nobody would notice that ten centuries on). Reclining figures of *Night* (a female figure sunk in sleep) and *Day* (a vigorous, muscular male figure in a rather strange and twisted position, the face incomplete) lie at each end of his sarcophagus. On the right, *Lorenzo*, wearing a helmet, sits nobly sunk in thought (he has in fact been nick-named "Il Pensieroso" or thinker). The reclining figures at his feet represent *Dawn* (a newly awakened girl – perhaps the finest and most famous statue of all) and *Dusk* (an old man, nodding wearily off to sleep). Above the sarcophagus containing the remains of Lorenzo the Magnificent and his brother Giuliano, killed in the Pazzi conspira-

▲ ▶ *The Tomb of Giuliano, Duke of Nemours, by Michelangelo* and *detail.*

completed ones are those of *Giuliano*, Duke of Nemours, and *Lorenzo,* Duke of Urbino, son of Piero the Unfortunate. The twin tombs are placed in the splendid architectural setting, with the marvellously idealised figures of the two men in Roman dress and armour sitting above the two sarcophagi, which are surmounted by the famous allegorical statues. Standing with one's back to the altar, *Giuliano's tomb* is on the left, (in reply to someone pointing out that the resents all-consuming Time that leads inexorably to death, to Hades; the middle band is the terrestrial sphere, and the upper one, more luminous, with the lunettes and the dome, the vault of Heaven. The sarcophagi seem rent in the centre by volutes surmounting the two urns, symbolically enabling the souls of the two dukes to flee the confines of space and time, to attain redemption in the domain of Eternity (the Madonna and Child).

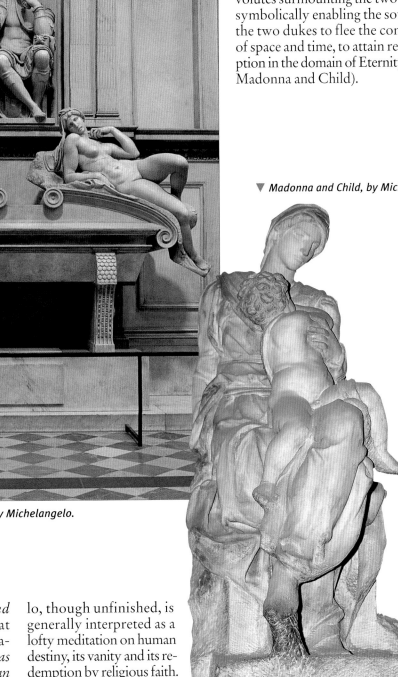

▼ *Madonna and Child, by Michelangelo.*

▲ *The Tomb of Lorenzo, Duke of Urbino, by Michelangelo.*

cy, is the beautiful *Madonna and Child*, also by Michelangelo, at which the two dukes contemplatively gaze; at the sides, *St. Cosmas* (left) by Montorsoli and *St. Damian* (right) by Raffaello da Montelupo, works by two pupils of Michelangelo that fall far below the expressive achievement of the statues near them. This work by Michelangelo, though unfinished, is generally interpreted as a lofty meditation on human destiny, its vanity and its redemption by religious faith. The three zones of the chapel can be understood in this sense: the lower order, with the tombs and allegorical statues, rep-

Night and *Day*, details of the Tomb of Giuliano, Duke of Nemours, by Michelangelo.

▲ ▼ *Dusk* and *Dawn, details of the Tomb of Lorenzo, Duke of Urbino, by Michelangelo.*

PALAZZO MEDICI-RICCARDI

Built for Cosimo the Elder between 1444 and 1460 by the Florentine architect and sculptor Michelozzo Michelozzi (a pupil of Ghiberti who worked with Donatello), this was the prototype of all Florentine palaces of the Renaissance. Majestic and elegant, it was filled with works of art commissioned by the Medici. The main branch of the family lived here until 1540. In 1655 the palace was sold to the Riccardi family and is now the seat of the provincial administration and the Prefecture. Exhibitions and other cultural events often take place here.

It was designed by Michelozzo as a large cube, and must have stood out among the lower buildings round it, but the Riccardi family had it enlarged, adding seven new windows. The two principal sides, have pronounced rustication on the ground floor, flatter rustication on the storey above and smooth stones on the third. This motif was to reappear frequently for more than a century, along with the use of twin-arched mullioned windows. There is a fine classical cornice, while the big corner windows (called "kneeling windows" from the form of the corbels) which replaced a previously

▲ *Palazzo Medici-Riccardi.*

▼ *Procession of the Magi on their Way to Betlehem, by Benozzo Gozzoli (c. 1460).*

▲ *The Gallery of Palazzo Medici-Riccardi, frescoed by Luca Giordano.*

existing loggia, are attributed to Michelangelo (c. 1517). On the same corner is a large *Medici coat of arms.* Inside the palace is a fine porticoed **Courtyard**, that contains Roman remains and various pieces of sculpture. This palace used to contain many of the masterpieces that are now on view in the galleries and museums of Florence. One of the most important items is the **Chapel** by Michelozzo, at the top of the first staircase on the right from the courtyard. Here are the celebrated frescoes by Benozzo Gozzoli representing the *Procession of the Magi on their Way to Bethlehem* (1459-60) in which many personages of the time are portrayed: Lorenzo the Magnificent with his father, Piero the Gouty and his sisters; Galeazzo Maria Sforza; Sigismondo Malatesta; John VII Paleologus, Emperor of Constantinople; the painter himself and his master, Fra Angelico. An interesting **Gallery**, reached by going up the second staircase on the right from the courtyard, was decorated with stuccoes and mirrors at the end of the 18th century, with a fine frescoed ceiling by Luca Giordano showing the *Apotheosis of the Medici Dynasty* (1682-83).

SAN MARCO

Piazza San Marco has a prevalently modern look; the only medieval note is the 14th century loggia of the Accademia; once part of the former Hospital of St. Matthew, and now the entrance portico of the Academy of Fine Arts. On the corner with Via degli Arazzieri is the **Palace of Livia** (1775), built by Grand Duke Pietro Leopoldo for a circus dancer, Livia Malfatti. In the centre of the piazza are shrubs and trees and a ***Monument to General Manfredo Fanti***, by Pio Fedi (1873).

One side of the piazza is occupied by the **Church** and **Monastery of San Marco**. There was a monastery of Salvestrini monks here from 1299 onwards; in the first half of the 15th century Cosimo the Elder assigned both the church and the monastery to the reformed Dominican monks of the Blessed Giovanni Dominici; this was partly by the desire of Pope Eugene IV, and partly in expiation of Cosimo's own misdeeds. He commissioned Michelozzo to carry out the work of restoration. In the following centuries there were several alterations, particularly to the church, which has now a late 18th century façade in a neo-cinquecento style.

The interior was re-structured by Giambologna in 1588 and by Silvani in 1678; on the interior façade is a *Crucifix* by followers of Giotto; at the third altar on the right, a *Virgin in prayer* (Mosaic).

◀ *The Cloister of Sant'Antonino, by Michelozzo.*

SAN MARCO MUSEUM

The entrance to the Monastery of San Marco is beside the church, one of the most important centres in Florence in the 15th century because of the protection granted to it by Cosimo the Elder and Lorenzo the Magnificent and also because of the unquestioned authority of its prior, Sant'Antonino. Savonarola, Fra Angelico and Fra Bartolomeo all lived there.

Fra Angelico was one of the greatest artists of the 15th century. He infused Masaccio's newly rediscovered rules of perspective with a spirit that was still Gothic, to express a mystical, contemplative religious experience.

The ***Cloister of Sant'Antonino***, by Michelozzo, has frescoed lunettes and some interesting rooms give onto it.

The ***Pilgrims' Hospice*** contains an exceptional series of panel paintings by Fra Angelico: the *Linen Merchant's Tabernacle*, the *Altarpiece from the Convent of Bosco ai Frati*, the *Annalena Altarpiece*, the *Descent from the Cross*, the *Last Judgement*.

▶ *Noli me tangere, by Fra Angelico.*

▲ *Annunciation, by Fra Angelico.*

The ***Chapter-house*** contains a magnificent *Crucifixion* by Fra Angelico. The artist also decorated the ***Dormitory*** on the first floor between 1439 and 1445; each cell, fascinating in its simplicity, is adorned with masterpieces, like the *Annunciation, Noli me tangere,* the *Transfiguration* and the *Coronation of the Virgin.*
In the ***Prior's Apartment*** is a *Portrait of Savonarola*, who lived here, by his disciple Fra Bartolomeo.

▶ *Last Judgement, by Fra Angelico.*

▼ *Deposition from the Cross,*
by Fra Angelico (c. 1435-40).

▼ *Imposition of the Name*
on the Baptist,
by Fra Angelico (1435).

▲ *Flight into Egypt, panel of the Door of the Silver Cupboard,*
by Fra Angelico.

·I·N·R·I·

▲ ◄ *The Church of Santissima Annunziata with the Monument to Grand Duke Ferdinando I, by Giambologna and the Cloister of Vows.*

In 1250, seven young Florentines, later beatified as the Seven Holy Founders, set up the order of the Servants of Mary, and began to build a shrine dedicated to the Virgin.

The church was rebuilt by Michelozzo in the 15th century and later by Antonio Manetti who, together with Leon Battista Alberti, was responsible for the design of the circular choir at the end of the aisleless nave.

The porch on the piazza is late 16th century. Between this and the church is the **Cloister of Vows**, decorated with fine early sixteenth-century frescoes by Andrea del Sarto, and other Mannerist artists.

To the left of the entrance, just inside the church (restored and embellished in the Baroque period) is a small 15th century *Temple*, that contains a greatly-venerated 13th century *Annunciation*, which is supposed to have been painted partly by an angel. Among the many works of art, mention should be made of two *lecterns* in the form of eagles (15th century English work). In the elegant tribune, *Jesus and St. Julian* by Andrea del Castagno (c. 1455, first altar on the left) and the *Trinity* by the same (second altar on the left).

Beside the church are the buildings of the **Monastery** which include the *Cloister of the Dead*, frescoed with *Stories of the Servants of Mary* by Florentine Mannerist artists.

SPEDALE DEGLI INNOCENTI

In 1419 the Guild of Silk Merchants decided to purchase a piece of land and build a hospital for foundlings or "Innocents". Brunelleschi was commissioned to provide the plan, which determined the architecture of the whole piazza onto which the hospital faces, creating a portico whose proportions, in relation to the rest, required the uniformity of all the surrounding buildings. We can see here how the Renaissance conception of "planning" replaced the casual building that went on in the Middle Ages, when one building was put up beside another in a completely different style. The hospital was finished in 1457.

The front consists of nine wide arches on columns that stand at the top of a flight of steps. Above these, a low upper storey which has windows with tympanums. Between the arches, glazed terra-cotta ton-

▲ *View of Piazza Santissima Annunziata
with the Spedale degli Innocenti
and one of the terra-cotta tondos,
by Andrea della Robbia, on the façade.*

dos of *babies in swadding clothes* by Andrea della Robbia (c. 1487). Two pilaster strips close the portico at the sides.

Inside, the exquisitely simple cloisters by Brunelleschi and a collection of works mostly of the 15th century. The collection includes: an *Annunciation* by Giovanni del Biondo; *Madonna and Child with Saints* by Piero di Cosimo; *Adoration of the Magi* by Ghirlandaio (1488); a *Madonna and Child with Angels* by the school of Perugino; the *Madonna of the Innocents*, attributed to Pontormo.

◀ *One of the cloisters of the
Spedale degli Innocenti, by Brunelleschi.*

ARCHAEOLOGICAL MUSEUM

Cosimo the Elder was a keen collector of coins, goldsmiths' work and antique sculpture, a passion shared by the later Medici. The Hapsburg-Lorraine family started the Egyptian antiquities section and encouraged independent excavation. In 1828 Leopold II subsidised an archaeological expedition in Egypt and Nubia, led by the Frenchman Champollion and the Italian Rossellini. In 1880 the collection was housed in its present seat, **Palazzo della Crocetta**, built by Giulio Parigi in 1820.

The museum is divided into three sections: the **Etrurian Topographical Museum**, the **Etrusco-Graeco-Roman Antiquities**, and the **Egyptian Museum**.

On the ground floor, the rooms are arranged didactically: the famous *François Vase* and the *Mater Matuta* are kept here. The pleasant garden contains reconstructions (partly with authentic materials) of funeral monuments and Etruscan tombs.

The Egyptian Museum is on the first floor. Among the most interesting exhibits: the two *statuettes of handmaidens* intent on domestic work; the *Statue of Thutmosis III* (1490-1436 BC); the *"Fayyum"*

▲ *The François vase, masterpiece of Greek ceramics (6th cent. BC).*

▶ *Mater Matuta, Italic goddess of fertility and maternity (5th cent. BC).*

Portrait of a Woman (2nd century AD); painted slabs, stelae, sarcophagi, mummies and a war chariot.

▼ *Egyptian stelae.*

Also on the first floor, among the Antiquities, *Attic kouroi* of the 6th century BC; Etruscan funeral urns; a *Statue of the Orator* (c. 100 BC); Etruscan sarcophagi; the *Chimera of Arezzo*; the *Little Idol*; Attic vases and Etruscan buccheri. Pre-Roman and Italic finds, along with those from Magna Grecia, are on the upper floors.

SYNAGOGUE

This marvellous temple, so prized by the Jewish community of Florence, was commenced in 1874 and was designed by the architects Treves, Falcini and Micheli. It was inaugurated on 24th October 1882. The construction of the monumental building was financed by a conspicuous fund bequeathed by David Levi, who had been the chairman of the Board of the Israelitic University of Florence from 1860 to 1870. The building is in pure Moorish style.

The interior is completely frescoed, while the *Ekhal* is covered with gleaming Venetian mosaic. Due to the predominatly Levantine Jewish origin of the Florentine community, the official rite is orthodox Sephardic, whilst the Ashkenazi minority meets in a room next-door to the Temple. The Synagogue was much damaged during the IInd World War and suffered further during the 1966 flood. The restoration has been carried out thanks to the contributions of the many visitors who daily flock to the Temple from all over the world.

▶ *The Synagogue.*

ACCADEMIA GALLERY

This is one of the most famous galleries in Italy, visited by thousands of people, especially owing to the presence of the *David* and of other famous sculptures by Michelangelo. The Gallery was founded in 1784 by Grand Duke Peter Leopold of Hapsburg Lorraine as an Academy of Fine Arts, to unite all the schools of art drawing and sculpture already existing in the city. The gallery was thus created with the specific purpose of helping the pupils to know and to study the Old Masters. Many of the pieces came, however, from a previous collection that belonged to the Academy of the Art of Drawing, an institution of great prestige, founded in 1562 by Cosimo I. This included all the greatest artists of the time, and was based on the fourteenth-century Company of Painters of St. Luke.

The already considerable collection of paintings was increased as a result of the suppression of churches and monasteries (1786 and 1808); there were further acquisitions and in 1873 the *David* was brought here, followed in 1911 by the *Prisoners* and *St. Matthew*, while the *Pietà* only arrived in 1939, when it was bought by the State. The Gallery also exhibits a plaster model of the *Rape of the Sabine Women* by Giambologna as well as a notable collection of paintings from the 13th till the early 16th century; among the most important works are: a *Crucifix*, Sienese school, second half of the 13th century

▶ *David, by Michelangelo*
and *detail*.

100

◀ *The Tribuna,*
by Emilio de Fabris.

◀ ▼ *Three*
of the four Prisoners,
by Michelangelo;
from the left:
the Young Prisoner,
the "Bearded" Prisoner
and the Prisoner
known as "Atlas".

◀ Saint Matthew, by Michelangelo.

(attributed by some to the great Duccio di Buoninsegna); the *Tree of Life*, by Pacino di Buonaguida (early 14th century); a *Polyptych* by Andrea Orcagna (mid 14th century) and works by his brothers, including a *Triptych* by Nardo di Cione (1365) and a *Coronation of the Virgin* by Jacopo di Cione; twenty-four panels by Taddeo Gaddi (fourteen with *Scenes of the Life of Christ* and ten with *Scenes of the Life of St. Francis*); the very fine *Pietà* by Giovanni da Milano (1365); the *Adimari Chest*; a *Visitation* attributed to Domenico Ghirlandaio; the *Madonna of the Sea* and the youthful *Madonna and Child, the Infant St. John and Two Angels*, by Sandro Botticelli; *Trinity and Saints*, by Alessio Baldovinetti (1471).

◀ The Palestrina Pietà, by Michelangelo.

◀ *Venus and Cupid,*
by Pontormo.

▶ *Madonna and Child,*
the Infant Saint John
and Two Angels,
by Sandro Botticelli.

▶ *The Tree of Life,*
by Pacino di Buonaguida.

▲ *Assumption of the Virgin, by Perugino.*

PIAZZA SANTA CROCE

From the Middle Ages onwards was the scene of festivities, tournaments, meetings, games; there was a famous tournament here between Lorenzo and Giuliano dei Medici. St. Bernardino da Siena preached here, the Florentine Carnival took place here, like the game of football in Renaissance costume. In 1865 Enrico Pazzi placed the *Monument to Dante* (later transferred to the front of the church) in the middle of the square.

On the south side of the piazza is **Palazzo dell'Antella**, the façade of which, on corbels, was frescoed in the space of three weeks by twelve painters directed by Giovanni da San Giovanni (17th century). A *Bust of Cosimo II* is above the door. Between two windows on the ground floor is a sixteenth-century marble disc indicating the centre of the piazza for the football game.

The classical façade of the Palazzo Cocchi-Serristori, opposite the church, is attributed to Baccio d'Agnolo (16th century).

▼ *"Calcio in costume",*
a folkloristic football game
that takes place every year in this square.

◀ *The Monument to Dante Alighieri,*
by Enrico Pazzi, located on the sagrato
of the Church of Santa Croce.

◀▼ *The fountain and*
detail of the façade of Palazzo dell'Antella,
in Piazza Santa Croce.

SANTA CROCE

This church originated as a small oratory, was built by a community of monks in 1228. In 1294 Arnolfo di Cambio began the construction of the present basilica, in the monumental, soberly decorated style that characterises Franciscan churches. The church was consecrated in 1443 in the presence of Pope Eugene IV. In 1566 Giorgio Vasari, commissioned by Cosimo I, designed the altars in the side aisles; this involved destroying the old choir and numerous frescoes. The façade of the church was only added in the mid 19th century and was designed by Niccolò Matas in neo-Gothic style (like the bell tower built by Gaetano Baccani in 1847). The extraordinary importance of this church, with its numerous art works, is enhanced by the many tombs of illustrious men (the "Urns of the Strong" celebrated by Ugo Foscolo in the *Sepolcri*).

The interior has a nave and two side aisles, with pointed arches supported by octagonal stone pillars. The floor is studded with no fewer than 276 tombstones, the oldest being 14th century. In the central nave, at

▼▲ *Façade of the Church of Santa Croce* and *detail of the disc in the tympanum with the plaque of Saint Bernardino.*

▲ ◄ *The interior of Santa Croce* and *the Pulpit, by Benedetto da Maiano.*

the third pillar on the right, is the fine marble *Pulpit* by Benedetto da Maiano (1472-76); the square panels relate *Episodes from the Life of St. Francis.* In the right aisle, at the first pillar, the *Madonna del Latte* by Rossellino (1478); opposite, the *Funeral Monument to Michelangelo* by Vasari and helpers (1570); the crouching female figures represent the *Muses of Painting, Sculpture* and *Architecture.* Next come the *Cenotaph of Dante Alighieri* (buried at Ravenna) by Stefano Ricci (1829); the *Tomb of Vittorio Alfieri,* by Canova in 1810; the *Monument to Niccolò Machiavelli,* by Spinazzi (1787); the splendid *Annunciation* by Donatello (c. 1435); the

▲ *Heraclius enters Jerusalem with the Cross, fresco of the Main Chapel, by Agnolo Gaddi.*

TANTO. NOMINI. NVLLVM. PAR. ELOGIVM

NICOLAVS. MACHIAVELLI

OBIT. AN. A.P. V. CIƆIƆXXVII.

▲ ► *Funeral Monuments to Niccolò Machiavelli,
by Innocenzo Spinazzi and to Michelangelo, by Giorgio Vasari.*

Monument to Leonardo Bruni, by Rossellino (c. 1444); the *Tomb of Gioacchino Rossini* and that of *Ugo Foscolo*. In the right transept, on the right, is the **Castellani Chapel**, frescoed about 1385 by Agnolo Gaddi with *Stories of St. Nicholas of Bari, John the Baptist* and *Anthony Abbot*. At the end of the transept is the entrance to the **Baroncelli Chapel**, frescoed with *Stories of the Virgin* by Taddeo Gaddi (1332-38); on the altar a polyptych with the *Coronation of the Virgin*, from the work-

shop of Giotto. At the corner of the transept is the entrance to the fine fourteenth-century **Sacristy**; on the right wall, three episodes from the *Passion* by Taddeo Gaddi and others; in the end wall is the entrance to the **Rinuccini Chapel,** with frescoes by Giovanni da Milano. Returning to the church, one should visit the chapels at the east end; the **Peruzzi Chapel** (fourth from the right) has splendid frescoes by Giotto with *Stories of the Baptist* and *St. John the Evangelist*. The **Bardi Chapel** (the fifth) has *Stories of St. Francis*, also by Giotto; this cycle is to be placed among the painter's masterpieces (c. 1325). The **Main Chapel** has frescoes by Agnolo Gaddi and a *Polyptych* by Niccolò

▼ **The Death of Saint Francis, by Giotto, in the Bardi Chapel.**

▲ *The Baroncelli Chapel, frescoed by Taddeo Gaddi.*

▲ ◀ The Sacristy
and *detail of the Crucifixion,*
by Taddeo Gaddi.

Gerini (late 14th century). Of the
left transept chapels, the **Bardi di
Vernio Chapel** has fine *Stories of St.
Sylvester*, by Maso di Banco (c.
1340). The Bardi Chapel at the head
of the transept has a *Crucifix* by Do-
natello (c. 1425).
On the left, the **Salviati Chapel** with
the nineteenth-century *tomb of Sofia
Zamoyska* by Lorenzo Bartolini.
The series of funeral monuments
continues in the left aisle; note the
Tomb of Carlo Marsuppini, by
Desiderio Settignano (c. 1453) and
that of *Galileo Galilei* by Giulio
Foggini (18th century).

▲ *The Main Cloister, entrance to the Pazzi Chapel.*

tury **Refectory**; the end wall is covered by an enormous fresco by Taddeo Gaddi representing the *Crucifix with the Tree of Life*, the *Last Supper* and other scenes; on the right wall is the grandiose *Crucifix* painted on wood by Cimabue, badly damaged by the flooding in 1966, and

▲ ▼ *Crucifix painted on wood, by Cimabue* and *gilded bronze statue of Saint Louis of Toulouse, by Donatello.*

Pazzi Chapel

On the right of the Church of Santa Croce are the buildings of the Franciscan monastery. The **Main Cloister** or **First Cloister** is against the wall of the right aisle; the porticoes are 14th-15th century; on the right of the entrance is the *Monument to Florence Nightingale*, (1820-1910), the heroic "Lady of the Lamp" who anticipated the work of the Red Cross on the battlefields and in the field hospitals during the Crimean War. At the end of the cloister appears the wonderful front of the Pazzi Chapel.

Filippo Brunelleschi designed the building and began it (it had the function of chapterhouse of the monastery and family burial chapel for the commissioners) about 1430: he worked on it at intervals until 1444, then other architects completed the building.

An atrium precedes the entrance: this has six Corinthian columns and a wide central arch; the frieze with *Heads of Cherubs* is by Desiderio da Settignano. The chapel has a dome with conical covering (1461) and under the atrium is another small dome in coloured terracotta, by Luca della Robbia; by the same, the *Tondo of St. Andrew* over the door, whose panels are splendidly carved by Giuliano da Maiano (1472).

The rectangular interior has the geometric limpidity and measured rhythm of the best creations of Brunelleschi: white walls, grooved pilaster strips in pietra serena, wide arches: the only touches of colour are the fine tondos by Luca della Robbia, with figures of *Apostles* and *Evangelists*. In the presbitery, a stained glass panel attributed to Alessio Baldovinetti and a small dome with *Signs of the Zodiac*.

Going out into the First Cloister, a doorway on the left leads into the **Large Cloister** or **Second Cloister** designed by Brunelleschi.

Museo dell'Opera di Santa Croce

This is housed in some of the rooms of the Monastery of Santa Croce. The first, and most important of these is the old 14th century

▲ *Crucifix with the Tree of Life and the Last Supper on the base, fresco by Taddeo Gaddi.*

three fragments of the *Triumph of Death* frescoed by Orcagna on the walls of Santa Croce (they were found under Vasari's altars, and detached); on the left is the statue in bronze of *St. Louis of Toulouse* by Donatello (1423). The remains of 14th and 15th century glass windows, the work of Andrea del Castagno, Agnolo Bronzino, Giorgio Vasari and others, are kept in the other rooms.

◄ *Detail of the Last Judgement, by Andrea Orcagna.*

PIAZZA SAN FIRENZE

Not far from Piazza della Signoria, and not very large, this piazza is dominated by two fine, large palaces of different epoch and style. One of these is **Palazzo Gondi,** by Giuliano da Sangallo (1490-1501). Opposite is the great building of the so-called **San Firenze,** the best Baroque in Florence (end of 17th and 18th century). Now the seat of the Tribunal, it incorporates the church of San Filippo Neri, known as San Firenze, with a fine Baroque interior.

▶ *The Bargello "Prison" in a 19th century paint.*

BARGELLO NATIONAL MUSEUM

This is the most important Italian museum of sculpture and minor arts. It is housed in the severe, square Palazzo del Bargello, a thirteenth-century building of great historical importance, that was begun in 1225 and was first used as the seat of the Captain of the People. After 1574 it was the seat of the Captain of Justice, or "Bargello" (that is the chief of police) and the palace became notorious for the executions held there. The Museum was founded in 1859.

A description of the principal works must begin with the splendid *Courtyard,* under the arches of which there is a large and very fine *cannon* of the early 17th century and, among the sculptures, the delightful *Fisherboy* by Vincenzo Gemito (1877). One of the rooms on the ground floor contains such masterpieces by

◀ *Palazzo del Bargello, seat of the National Museum.*

115

▲ *The Courtyard with the staircase by Neri di Fioravante.*

▼ *View of the northern portico.*

◄ Madonna and Child and the Young Saint John, by Michelangelo, know as the "Pitti Tondo".

Michelangelo as the *Bust of Brutus* (1539), who was seen at that time as a heroic liberator from tyranny, the so-called *Pitti Tondo* (c. 1504), rendered with the characteristic and expressive "unfinished" style; the *David-Apollo* (c. 1531), delicate and harmonious; and the youthful *Drunken Bacchus* (1496-97).

▼ Drunken Bacchus, by Michelangelo (1496).

▲ Bust of Cosimo I dei Medici, by Benvenuto Cellini.

In the same room we have another *Bacchus* by Sansovino (1520) and the bronze *Bust of Cosimo I*, exquisitely modelled by Benvenuto Cellini (1545-47), as well as Giambologna's famous *Mercury*.
On the first floor, on the fine **balcony**, are more bronzes by Giambologna. In the **Donatello Hall**, besides masterpieces by the great fifteenth-century sculptor, are numerous terra-cotta works by Luca della Robbia and the panels with the *Sacrifice of Isaac* by Brunelleschi and Ghiberti.

◄ David-Apollo, by Michelangelo.

► Lady with
a bouquet
of flowers,
by Verrocchio.

▲ *Abraham sacrificing Isaac*, by Lorenzo Ghiberti
and *Abraham sacrificing Isaac*, by Filippo Brunelleschi.

► *Mercury,*
by Cellini.

◄ *David*, by Donatello
and *David*, by Verrocchio.

118

The other rooms display splendid majolica pottery from Faenza and other provenances, enamels, goldsmiths' work, liturgical objects and valuable ivories of various periods.

On the second floor: a room with terra-cotta items by Giovanni della Robbia and one with those by his father Andrea; a room devoted to Verrocchio that also contains lovely works by Laurana, Mino da Fiesole, Benedetto Maiano, Rossellino and Pollaiolo; lastly, two rooms with small bronzes (and a huge, stupendous 15th century fireplace) and arms.

◀ *Madonna of Humility, from Andrea della Robbia's workshop.*

▼ *Madonna and Child with Angels, polychrome terra-cotta relief, by Antonio Rossellino.*

◀ *13th century Limousin Reliquiary Casket in wood and enamelled copper, with pyramid-shaped lid.*

▲ *13th century Limoges enamelled copper Reliquiary Casket.*

PIAZZALE MICHELANGELO

On the south side of the Arno, going along Viale Michelangelo or else walking up the ramps that go up from the San Niccolò gate, one comes to a large panoramic terrace, which affords a view over the whole town and the surrounding hills: Piazzale Michelangelo. This large area was conceived by Giuseppe Poggi in the 1860's as the scenographic climax to his work of "redesigning" the town; Florence was then the capital of Italy. In the centre of the square is a copy of the *David* commemorating Michelangelo. Going on up the hill, behind Piazzale Michelangelo, is the beautiful little **Church of San Salvatore al Monte**, designed by Cronaca in 1499. Inside there appears for the first time in the Renaissance a double order of columns, superimposed.

▲ *The Monument to Michelangelo with the bronze copy of the David, at the centre of the square.*

One of the oldest and most beautiful churches in Florence. A wide marble staircase leads up to it from nearby Piazzale Michelangelo. An ancient oratory, dedicated to St. Minias, reputedly martyred on that hill in the 4th century, was incorporated into the Romanesque church between the 11th and 13th century.

The façade is faced with green and white marble. The fine mosaic in the centre (13th century) represents *Christ between the Virgin and St. Minias*; at the top of the tympanum, an *Eagle*, symbol of the Guild of Woolmerchants who subsidised the upkeep of the church.

The interior has a nave and two side aisles, with a crypt and a raised presbytery above it. The floor of the nave is inlaid with splendid marble panels. In the centre, between the two flights of steps leading up to the presbytery, is the ***Crucifix Chapel*** by Michelozzo (1448), commissioned by Piero the Gouty, with a delightful multicoloured timbered and majolica vault by Luca della Robbia and altar panels by Agnolo Gaddi. From the left aisle one enters the ***Chapel of the Cardinal of Portugal***, one of the most elegant creations of the Florentine Renaissance, by Antonio Manetti (1461-66), a pupil of Brunelleschi; this contains the *Tomb of Jacopo di Lusi-*

▼ *Tomb of Jacopo di Lusitania, archbishop of Lisbon, by Antonio Rossellino.*

▼ *The splendid Church of San Miniato on the hill known as "Monte alle Croci", behind Piazzale Michelangelo.*

tania, archbishop of Lisbon, by Rossellino; fine della Robbia terracottas on the vault, a splendid *Annunciation* by Baldovinetti (on the left) and two *Angels* frescoed by Antonio and Piero del Pollaiolo. On the vault of the crypt, above the altar, are frescoes of *Saints and Prophets* by Taddeo Gaddi. The presbytery of the church is surrounded with a fine thirteenth-century marble transenna and a splendid *Pulpit*; on the right altar is a painting on wood by Jacopo del Casentino with *St. Minias and Eight Scenes from his Life*. The mosaic in the apse represents *Christ Enthroned between the Virgin, St. Minias and the Symbols of the Evangelists* (1279, but restored in 1491 by Baldovinetti). From the presbytery one turns right into the *Sacristy*, frescoed after 1387 by Spinello Aretino, with *Stories of St. Benedict*.

To the right of the church is the **Bishops' Palace** (13th to 14th century). Round the church are the *Walls* of the Fortress constructed by Michelangelo in 1529 to defend Florence during the siege by the Spanish army of Charles V.

▼ *The apse with the mosaic of Christ Enthroned between the Virgin, Saint Minias and the Symbols of the Evangelitsts.*

▲ ▶ Two views of Forte Belvedere.

Perched on the top of the hill of St. George, the fort is the highest point in Florence, and the splendid views one enjoys from its parapets in all directions fully justify the Fort's name of Belvedere (beautiful view). Already envisaged as a fort in the Duke of Athens' time, before his expulsion from Florence, it was finally commenced in 1590 by the famous military engineer Bernardo Buontalenti upon order of Ferdinand Ist de' Medici. The fort was designed to defend the city from the South and to protect the grand-ducal family in times of civil unrest. The governor of the Fort's residence is now used for internationally renowned exhibitions.

FIESOLE

A charming little town about five miles north of Florence, it was founded by the Etruscans in the 7th century BC. Three centuries later it was colonised by the Romans. After the fall of the Empire it was an important bishopric; then in the 12th century it succumbed to its stronger neighbour, Florence. After losing all its political power, it became a favourite summer resort for rich Florentines (the Medicis had a villa here) and in the 18th century foreign visitors, especially the English, also came here.

The centre of the little town is the wide **Piazza Mino**, where are the principal public buildings.

The **Cathedral** was built in 1028 and later enlarged. In the *Salutati*

▲ *Piazza Mino da Fiesole.*

Chapel are frescoes by Cosimo Rosselli and the *Tomb of the Bishop Leonardo Salutati*, by Mino da Fiesole (15th century). On the high altar is a *Triptych* by Bicci di Lorenzo (c. 1440). In the crypt, which is Romanesque, are fifteenth-century frescoes by Benedetto di Nanni, a *Baptismal Font* by Francesco del Tadda (16th century) and the *Wooden Bishop's Chair of St. Andrea Corsini* (14th century).

The **Bandini Museum** nearby has interesting Della Robbia terracottas and works by Agnolo and Taddeo Gaddi, Lorenzo Monaco and Jacopo del Sellaio. Also in Piazza Mino is the **Praetorian Palace** (15th century) with façade and loggia covered with *coats of arms*.

Near the piazza is the **Roman Theatre** (1st century AD) which seats an audience of 3000 and is still in use for summer concerts and other events. In the vicinity of the theatre are the remains of a *Temple* (first Etruscan and later Roman) and some *Roman baths*.

◀ *The façade of the Cathedral.*

▲ ◄ *The Roman Theatre*
and *the Church of San Francesco.*

The **Archaeological Museum** beside the area of excavation contains relics of Etruscan and Roman Fiesole; urns from Chiusi and Volterra; storied stelae, typical of the zone; Greek vases, objects in bucchero, small bronzes and other sculptures. Returning to the piazza, one goes up a very steep little road to **Sant'Alessandro,** an ancient church standing on the site of an Etruscan temple. A little beyond it are the **Church** and **Monastery of San Francesco;** this church was built between the 14th and 15th century, and has a simple façade with a rose window and porched entrance. The interior is Gothic with a single nave; the high altar has a beautiful *Annunciation* by Raffaellino del Garbo (early 16th century); at the second altar on the left, *Madonna and Saints* by the school of Perugino; next to it, an *Immaculate Conception* by Cosimo Rosselli. The fine inlaid *choir* is early 16th century. Right of the church is the small **Cloister of St. Bernardino** (13th to 14th century).

Half way between Fiesole and Florence is the **Church of San Domenico** built in the 15th century but restored in the 17th; it contains a *Madonna and Child with Angels and Saints* (c. 1430) by Fra Angelico, who was prior of the nearby monastery.

INDEX